DETECTIVE'S HANDBOOK

Illustrated by Colin King

Contributors:
Anne Civardi, Judy Hindley,
Angela Wilkes, Donald Rumbelow,
and Heather Amery

About this book

Detective work is very difficult, but very exciting. To be a good detective you must be patient, watchful and well-trained. You must know how to build the whole story of a crime from tiny clues. But you must also be ready to spring into action at any time – poised to pounce on even the sneekiest criminal.

That is what this book is all about. It shows you the special skills detectives use, such as identifying fingerprints and handwriting, questioning witnesses, and reading clues. It tells you what information you need in order to act fast in emergencies.

You'll find games, puzzles and training courses to help you try things out. And there are lots of stories about the kinds of tricks crooks play – so you'll be prepared for them when you meet them.

This edition first published in 2008 by Usborne Publishing Ltd., Usborne House, 83-85 Saffron Hill, London EC1N 8RT, England. www.usborne.com. Copyright © Usborne Publishing Ltd 2008, 1989, 1978. The name Usborne and the devices ♀ ⊕ are Trade Marks of Usborne Publishing Ltd. All rights reserved.

Contents

Detective work

Good detectives are quick-witted, sharp-eyed and always on the look-out for anything suspicious. They must learn to do all sorts of things, such as looking for clues, questioning people and tracking suspects. Here are some ways to make the grade.

Make sure you look everywhere when searching for clues.

Remember, the most unlikely things may be important clues.

Even the craftiest crook may leave a clue at the scene of a crime.

Check everything you find very carefully. It may lead you to the villain.

Train yourself to remember the faces of suspicious characters.

You never know where you may see them again, sometimes much later.

Wear clothes that blend in when you are tracking a crook.

Tiptoe very quietly and try and get as close to him as possible.

Be careful to question people who saw a crook in action. They are called witnesses.

If you see someone who is acting suspiciously, don't be afraid to ask him what he is doing.

Setting up an office

Before you can do any detective work, you need an office to work from. Here you can store your detective gear and set up crafty traps for crooks. Some may help you to guess if a suspect is innocent or guilty. Look at Detective Dodd's office to get some tips.

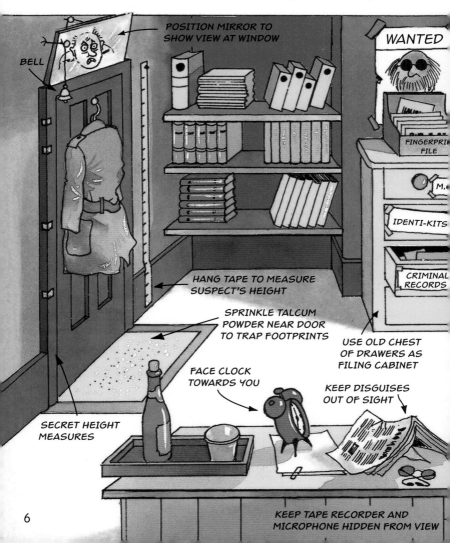

POSITION MIRROR TO SHOW VIEW AT WINDOW

WANTED

BELL

FINGERPRINT FILE

M.

IDENTI-KITS

CRIMINAL RECORDS

HANG TAPE TO MEASURE SUSPECT'S HEIGHT

SPRINKLE TALCUM POWDER NEAR DOOR TO TRAP FOOTPRINTS

USE OLD CHEST OF DRAWERS AS FILING CABINET

FACE CLOCK TOWARDS YOU

KEEP DISGUISES OUT OF SIGHT

SECRET HEIGHT MEASURES

KEEP TAPE RECORDER AND MICROPHONE HIDDEN FROM VIEW

Sit with your back to the window, so when you question a suspect, you can see their face. Hang something above the door which makes a noise when the door is opened. Make sure you can also see if anything is going on behind you.

LOCAL AREA MAP

WANTED

REPORTS

RECENT CRIMES

SIT WITH BACK TOWARDS WINDOW

SECRET FOOT ALARM BUTTON

TELEPHONE BOOK

Give-aways

Even if he is in disguise, a crook may give himself away by a habit, such as pulling his ears or scratching his knees. Here are some of the different habits people have, which may help you to recognize a crook.

Whistling

Drumming fingers

Biting fingernails

Cracking knuckles

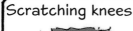
Scratching knees   Tapping feet   Wrapped legs

Biting glasses

Stroking beard

Twirling moustache

Twitch and tugging eyebrows

Picking teeth

Chewing gum

Grinding teeth

Pulling earlobe

Spot the clues

A cunning thief has robbed this room. The picture below shows what the room looked like before the burglary. The picture on the right is the same room after the crime has taken place.

How many clues can you spot? What has been stolen? Has anything been replaced with a fake? How many things have been disturbed?

You should be able to find at least 20 clues.

Hijack

Detectives have been tipped off that four dangerous crooks are planning to hijack a boat to escape the country. Quickly they set up a clever trap to catch them. Wearing disguises, the detectives take up their positions. They have been after this gang for many months. Now is their big chance to catch them. Can you work out how they do it?

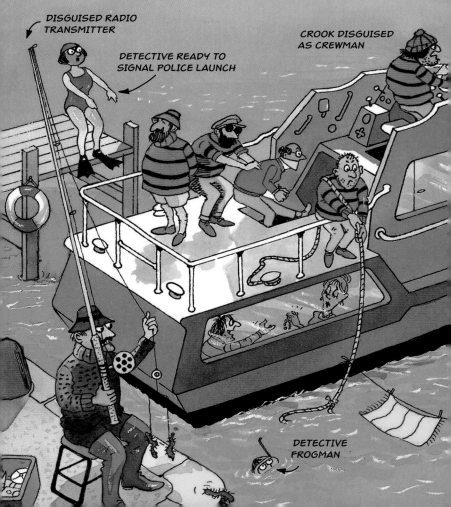

DISGUISED RADIO TRANSMITTER

DETECTIVE READY TO SIGNAL POLICE LAUNCH

CROOK DISGUISED AS CREWMAN

DETECTIVE FROGMAN

POLICE HELICOPTER

POLICE LAUNCH READY FOR ACTION

DETECTIVE FROGMEN

DETECTIVES DISGUISED AS FISHERMEN

DETECTIVE DISGUISED AS TOURIST

What happens

While the fishermen block the boat, a frogman jams its propellers with rope. Then the diver signals the police launch to swoop. The fisherman on the quay, using a radio disguised as a fishing rod, radios the helicopter to fly closer and lower men on to the deck. The crooks are arrested.

13

How crooks work

Some crooks stick to the same sort of crime and do it the same way each time. This is called their 'Modus Operandi' (M.O.) or way of working.

Good detectives keep a special M.O. file in their

Bones

Bones gives the guard dog a juicy bone when he robs a house. This keeps it quiet and happy.

Brusher

Brusher is very tidy. He always washes away his foot and finger prints after a crime.

Fred the Feet

Before each job, Fred the Feet removes his shoes and socks. But his footprints give him away.

Stuffer

This crook is nicknamed Stuffer because he eats so much. He drops bits of food wherever he goes.

office. Sometimes they give each crook a nickname to help them remember how he works and to catch him quickly. Here are the M.O.s of some crooks who burgle houses.

Gumboy

Every time he blows open a safe, Gumboy uses bubblegum to stick explosives to the safe door.

Pyramid Pete

Pyramid Pete always lays a trap in the house he burgles. This is to trip up the owner.

Junior

Junior brings his mother along to keep watch. But she leaves bits of embroidery behind.

The Count

The Count only robs very rich households. He pretends to be the owner of each house he robs.

Break-in

Late one night, a watch and jewel shop is robbed.
At the scene of the crime, Detective Trapper searches
for clues. Careful not to disturb anything, he circles
the room and makes a note of everything he sees.

Searching for clues

Don't touch anything with your
fingertips until the room has
been dusted for fingerprints.

Look for prints on drawers and
windows. But use a stick or ruler
to open and close them.

The villain has escaped with a sackful of diamond rings and watches, but he or she has been clumsy. How many tell-tale clues can you spot? Turn the page to see what evidence Detective Trapper finds.

Search everywhere. Even the smallest clues can help to identify a crook.

Always carry a notepad with you, so you can jot down everything witnesses tell you.

Gathering evidence

As soon as the shop is dusted for prints, Detectives Trapper and Dodd get down to work. They collect clues which will help them to catch the crook. Each piece of evidence is put in a plastic bag and carefully marked. Later it will go to the lab for examination.

The hairs on this comb may tell you what shade of hair the crook has, or if it's dyed.

An electric drill is found near the safe. But it's had the serial number filed off.

Dodd photographs a footprint on the carpet. He notices strange marks across it.

Trapper collects soil from the footprint for examination. It may show where the crook has been.

The crook left a message. Trapper measures it to get an idea of how tall the crook is.

As the crook climbed through the window, a few threads from his jacket caught on a nail.

Dodd uses a brush and powder to show up a set of fingerprints which will be photographed.

The M.O. file may record which crooks cut holes in the window glass to reach the latch inside.

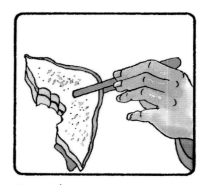

The crook may be traced through teethmarks found on a sandwich that was left behind.

Dodd examines the plastic sandwich wrapper. But he should pick it up with tweezers.

At the lab

BRUCE BUNGLE (THE SUSPECT)

EXAMINING DRILL UNDER INFRARED LAMP

SUSPECT'S M.O. FILE

B. BUNGLE M.O.

TESTING SOIL FROM SUSPECT'S SHOES

EXAMINING THREADS

At the lab, a team of experts examine all the evidence from the robbery very carefully. It looks as if the well-known but clumsy Bruce Bungle has been stealing again. So Bruce has been brought in for questioning and has his photo taken for the criminal record files.

Bruce must be the burglar because . . .
1. Soil from his shoes matches the soil found on the shop carpet.
2. The cuts in his shoe soles match those in the footprint photos.
3. A plaster cast of the sandwich show that the teethmarks in the snack match Bruce's.

SUSPECT'S DENTAL RECORDS

SNACK WRAPPER

4. Bruce's bleached hair is exactly the same as the hairs found on the comb.

5. The threads match the material of his jacket.

6. His M.O. file reveals that he leaves messages after a crime, and cuts glass out of a window to break in.

7. The serial number on the drill shows up in a special light, and so the shop that sold it to Bruce can now be traced.

8. Fingerprints on the glass are Bruce's.

9. Another puzzle is solved – the prints on the sandwich wrapper belong to Detective Dodd.

21

Is this the crook?

Crooks often try to change their looks. But their faces, feet and clothes sometimes give them away. A good detective looks carefully for things that will give clues about a person. What can you learn about the man below?

His hair is dyed, as the roots are black. He has shaved off his beard – the skin underneath is paler than the rest of his face. His rumpled clothes may mean he's been sleeping outside. Perhaps he's on the run from prison.

He wears his watch on his right wrist, so he may be left-handed. His broken nose may mean he is a boxer. His suit and shoes are too small – perhaps he has stolen them. The tattoo on his left hand may indicate that he is a sailor.

Things to look out for

This man wears glasses – look at the mark on his nose. His even, white teeth are probably false.

This man wears a hat – perhaps he wears a uniform at work. The scar on his cheek is new.

This woman is married and writes with her left hand. She takes great care of her hands and nails.

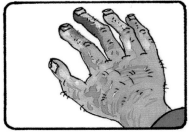

This man works with his hands. He obviously bites his nails, so he's probably a nervous person.

This man looks as if he rides a bicycle. The pencils in his pocket may mean he does paperwork.

Feet often give people away. Tall people usually have big feet, while short people have small ones.

Training dogs

Dogs often help detectives in their work. Petal is being trained to track down and catch crooks. She was chosen for detective work because she is a brave and clever dog. Before she can go out on patrol, Petal must learn to do whatever her handler tells her – on and off a lead, before and after a chase. It will take many months of hard training.

Petal first learns to walk to 'heel' beside her handler's left knee, like this.

Then she is trained to obey different orders, such as 'stand', 'sit' and 'lie down'.

If her handler tells her to 'stay', she mustn't move until she's told to 'come'.

An important lesson she learns is how to fetch things for her handler. This is called 'retrieving'.

If she's ordered to 'speak', Petal must bark. She should stop when told to be 'quiet'.

Petal is trained to climb up things which are too high to jump. This is one of the hardest exercises.

In case she has to chase a crook, Petal must know how to jump over low things like walls and logs.

Petal must be very fit and move quickly. She is taught how to leap across wide obstacles.

Petal is a very good swimmer and learns how to fetch things that are floating in the water.

She mustn't be afraid of loud noises. Sometimes crooks start shouting when they're arrested.

Nosework

Petal uses her nose to sniff out suspects – this is called nosework. She can smell and hear much better than a person can.

1. PETAL SNIFFS GLOVE DROPPED BY CROOK TO GET USED TO HIS SCENT

2. PICKS UP TRAIL AND JUMPS HEDGE HERE

3. LOSES SCENT CROSSING PATH BECAUSE SCENT OF RECENT WALKE IS STRONGER THA CROOK'S

4. PICKS UP CROOK'S SCENT AGAIN ON PIECE OF HIS SHIRT

5. CROSSES FIELD. IS NOT DISTRACTED BY SHEEP AND NOISY TRACTOR

Catching the suspect

If the suspect keeps still, Petal circles around him, growling.

If he tries to escape, she grips his arm and holds on with her teeth.

A crook is on the run. This picture shows how Petal picks up his scent. Follow the trail to find out where the crook is hiding.

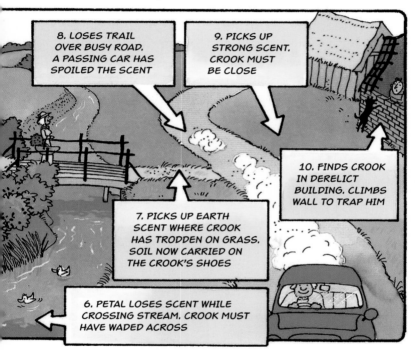

8. LOSES TRAIL OVER BUSY ROAD. A PASSING CAR HAS SPOILED THE SCENT

9. PICKS UP STRONG SCENT. CROOK MUST BE CLOSE

10. FINDS CROOK IN DERELICT BUILDING. CLIMBS WALL TO TRAP HIM

7. PICKS UP EARTH SCENT WHERE CROOK HAS TRODDEN ON GRASS. SOIL NOW CARRIED ON THE CROOK'S SHOES

6. PETAL LOSES SCENT WHILE CROSSING STREAM. CROOK MUST HAVE WADED ACROSS

Petal barks to let her handler know where she has cornered the crook.

The handler arrives and arrests the suspect. Petal can now sit and rest.

Framed (A case of false evidence)

Krusties, the well-known art dealers, are holding their yearly auction in two days' time. A very valuable painting is to be sold. Larry Loyal, Audrey Applecart and Harold Hoe, who work for Krusties, are the only three who know about the painting. They have arrived to collect it from its owner, Sir Timothy Trumble.

Inside Sir Timothy's stately home, Larry Loyal slips another painting over the real one to disguise it.

He is watched by Harold Hoe, Audrey Applecart and Sir Timothy Trumble as he does this.

Larry takes the painting home to guard it until the auction. He hangs it above his fireplace.

But, during the night, the painting is stolen. Detective Trapper arrives to investigate the crime.

The four suspects

Back in his office, Trapper looks at all the clues he found at the scene of the crime. He thinks carefully: "Four people knew where the painting was and one must be the thief. But who is it?"

Sir Timothy Trumble

Has he stolen the painting to claim the insurance money? And kept the painting as well?

Larry Loyal

Larry works hard, but doesn't make much money. Did he steal the painting to sell it?

Audrey Applecart

Audrey lives alone with her dog. She's a bit of a mystery and nobody knows much about her.

Harold Hoe

Harold has worked at Krusties for a many years. He's got a stiff leg because of an accident.

29

Misleading evidence

After questioning the four suspects, Trapper is sure that Sir Timothy is not the thief. He flew to Africa before the painting disappeared. And Larry must be innocent. His feet are much bigger than the prints found. All the evidence points to Harold Hoe . . .

"Your hat and footprints were found at Larry's house," Trapper tells Harold. "You must have stolen the painting."

"But I wasn't there" pleads Harold. "Wait, I remember. I lost some things when my house was robbed last month."

Is Harold telling the truth? Trapper looks in his crime complaints book to check that the burglary was reported.

Sure enough, it was. Among the stolen things were a hat and a pair of old shoes. Has Harold Hoe been framed?

Trapper returns to Larry's house. "Harold is too fat to get through that window, and he couldn't climb this wall with his stiff leg. And where are his walking stick marks? Just a minute — these are dog prints. Ah! Miss Applecart has a dog."

As he expected, Trapper finds the painting at Audrey's house. She confesses, "Yes, I robbed Harold's house. Then I wore his

shoes and left his hat behind when I stole the painting. I hoped I would mislead you and you would arrest Harold."

Which is the getaway car?

One evening, a crook smuggled a case full of gold watches through customs at a big airport. Five people saw him drive off in a green car.

A customs officer said that the car had a dent on the right wing. The steering wheel was on the left. The letters L and S and the number 2 were somewhere on the numberplate. He was also certain that the left headlight was broken.

An old lady thought that Y, K and a 4 were on the numberplate. The car had two doors.

A boy scout said that a front hub cap was missing. The car had four doors.

A businessman stated that the dent was on the left side. The right headlight was broken.

A porter thought the car had two side mirrors, one windshield wiper and an aerial on the roof.

The customs officer, the boy scout and the porter were right. The old lady and the businessman were wrong. So which of these eight cars do you think was the getaway car?

Answer

Car number 3 is the getaway car.

Detective disguises

Crooks often meet to talk about crimes or to hand over stolen goods. You may have to disguise yourself to get close enough to listen to their plans. Always wear clothes that go with your surroundings so the crooks don't notice you or get suspicious. A hat, dark glasses or a false moustache are useful disguises.

1 Gardener

If the crooks meet in a park, pretend to be a gardener. As you weed, try to get as close as you can to their meeting spot.

2

To get very close, use a pointed stick to pick up leaves and paper. Drop paper behind you if you want to go back again.

1 Window cleaner

To disguise yourself as a window cleaner, you need a bucket of water and a cloth. Remember to wear overalls or old clothes.

2

Move from one window to the next while you watch the crooks. But don't stare for too long as they might get suspicious.

Disguise yourself as a tourist if the crooks meet in a hotel or club. Hold a camera and map.

Pace up and down to get closer. Look at your watch as if you're waiting for someone.

Pretend to be jogging if you want to follow a crook. But don't get too close behind him.

If he suddenly turns around, pretend to do some leg and arm exercises or jog on the spot.

If the crooks meet in a crowded place, just hang around, look relaxed and listen.

You can pretend to be a street cleaner, while all the time watching and listening carefully.

On the look-out

Lord and Lady Tutton have invited all their rich friends to a summer ball. While everyone is dancing, a gang of crooks, disguised as guests and waiters, steal everything they can. Can you spot the eleven crooks and see how they're hiding the stolen things?

Door-to-door villains

Detectives are always on the look-out for crooks pretending to be drain inspectors or meter readers (1), or crooks who collect for fake charities (2), or sell stolen goods (3).

Suspicious cars

NEW SCREWS

Watch out for some of the following things. (1) An old car with new screws on the number plate may be stolen. (2) A van with no name on it. (3) A car full of men waiting near or outside a bank.

Identi-flick book

Make this flick book and use it when you question a witness. Ask the witnesses to flick over the strips until they find a face that looks most like the suspect's. The face changes a little each time you turn a strip over.

On the next four pages there are lots of different-shaped noses, eyes, mouths and chins to draw in the flick book.

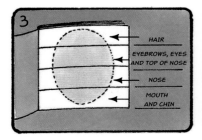

To make the book, pin or staple about 12 big pieces of paper together, like this.

Leave the two outside pages as covers. Cut the ten inside pages into four equal strips.

Strip 1 is for the hair, 2 for the eyes, eyebrows and top of the nose. 3 is for the nose, 4 for the mouth and the chin.

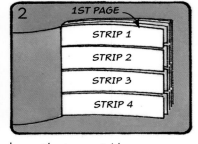

Draw a face on the four strips of the first page, with each part of the face on the correct strip. Draw in the ears as well.

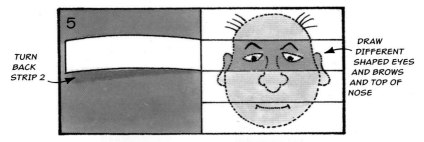

Turn back strip 2 and draw different shaped eyes on the next page.
Match up the top of a new nose with the bottom of the nose on page
one. Match up the ears and the outline of the face.

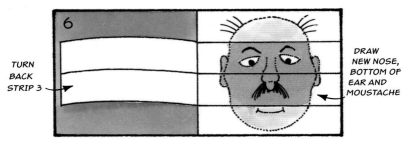

Turn back strip 3 of the first page and draw a different shaped nose
on the next page. Try drawing in a moustache as well. Match up the
ears and then draw in the outline of the face.

To finish off the second face, turn back strips 1 and 4 and then draw
a new hairstyle, mouth and chin. Keep turning the strips in this order
until you have drawn a face on every page.

Know your crook

Watch out for crooks who have disguised themselves. Just by growing a moustache or beard, by dyeing their hair or changing their hairstyle they may look quite different. Look how this man and woman change.

Identi-words

Hair

STRAIGHT AND BLONDE

CURLY AND SHORT

BALD

WAVY AND RED

GREASY, LANK AND BLACK

BROWN WITH FRINGE

Eyebrows

BUSHY

ARCHED

JOINED

SLANTING

STRAIGHT

NARROW

The identi-words below will help you describe a person quickly and properly. Write them down in your notebook and learn them off by heart if you can. Try making up some identi-words of your own too.

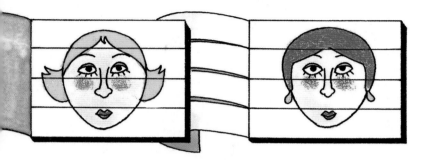

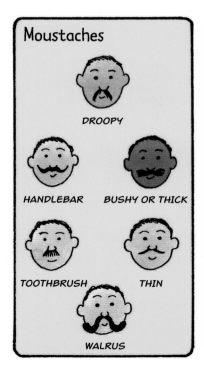

Moustaches

DROOPY

HANDLEBAR

BUSHY OR THICK

TOOTHBRUSH

THIN

WALRUS

Beards

POINTED

LONG

STUBBLY

BUSHY AND CURLY

SHORT

STRAGGLY

Identi-words

When you spot a suspect, ask yourself these questions to help you remember exactly what he or she looks like. What shape is the face and the chin, the mouth and the nose? What's the hair like?

Don't stare at the suspect for too long. Look quickly two or three times and jot down the answers as soon as you get the chance. Use these identi-words when you write your notes.

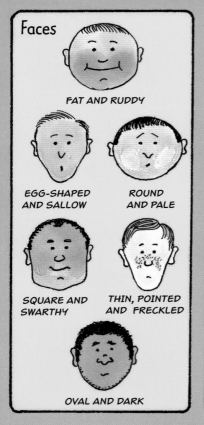

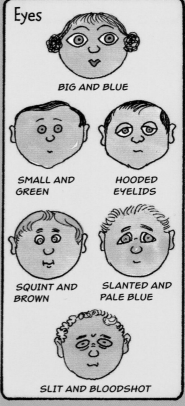

Mouths

FULL

THIN AND SMALL   CROOKED

UPTURNED   DOWN TURNED

WIDE

Chins

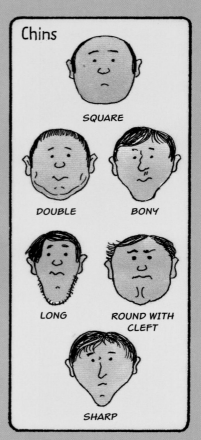

SQUARE

DOUBLE   BONY

LONG   ROUND WITH CLEFT

SHARP

Noses

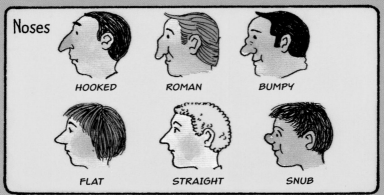

HOOKED   ROMAN   BUMPY

FLAT   STRAIGHT   SNUB

Identi-sketches

Look carefully at the suspect's shape and size. If you have time, make a quick sketch of him or her and describe each part of their body with identi-words. Note whether they're big or small, fat or thin, tall or short, and what clothes they're wearing.

Remember – they may try to disguise themselves by wearing different clothes.

EGG-SHAPED FACE

FULL LIPS

SHORT AND STOUT

WALKED WITH A LIMP

BLONDE CURLY HAIR

BIG GREEN EYES

BUMPY NOSE

CLEFT CHIN

SMARTLY DRESSED

BIG FEET

Look for unusual things, such as a limp or scar, that may help you recognize a suspect when you see them again some other time.

Remembering a suspect

AH YES. . . HE WAS SMALL, THIN AND WIRY LOOKING.

IDENTI BOOK
. . . IDENTI WORDS

HIS FACE . . . I REMEMBER NOW. IT WAS THIN AND BONY WITH A SHARP CHIN. THERE WAS SOMETHING STRANGE ABOUT HIS EYES. DID HE SQUINT?

Shapes and sizes

FAT

THIN AND TALL

STOUT

STOOPED

SMALL

Clothes

SMART

CASUAL

FLASHY

SHABBY

SPORTY

THAT'S IT . . . HIS NOSE WAS BIG AND HOOKED, HIS MOUTH MEAN AND CROOKED AND HE HAD DARK, GREASY HAIR. I'M SURE HE HAD A SCAR ON HIS LEFT CHEEK OR WAS IT HIS RIGHT?

I'VE SEEN HIM BEFORE SOMEWHERE QUITE RECENTLY . . . OF COURSE, I REMEMBER NOW . . . IT'S CROSS-EYED CHARLIE.

ven at night, a good detective is prepared for action
eady to investigate crimes and track down suspects.
There are lots of crooks who only work after dark.

One night, when Detectives Trapper and Dodd are
n duty, the telephone rings . . .

rapper grabs the telephone. He
s told that three suspicious
haracters were seen going into
he Clikon Camera warehouse.

Quickly, he and Dodd put on brown
coats. They wear soft-soled shoes
so that they can creep about
quietly in the dark.

hey collect all the equipment
hey will need, such as lights,
adios, handcuffs and infrared
noculars to see in the dark.

Petal is coming too, just in case
she can help. She may have to
sniff out the crooks and chase
after them if they run away.

Silently, Trapper pulls up outside the warehouse with the car lights off. He signals to everyone to keep very quiet.

He blocks the alley with the car to stop the crooks from getting away. Then he tells everyone to take up their positions.

Dodd uses his binoculars to keep watch. Trapper creeps around the building to check for escape routes and getaway cars.

Petal and her handler stay behind to guard the fire escape. The crooks could use it as a quick escape route.

Around a corner, Trapper finds a suspicious car. Is it waiting for the crooks to use? He radios HQ to check the number.

At HQ the police use computers to trace the car. Sure enough, it was stolen a week ago and they let Trapper know immediately.

The sting

Trapper and Dodd quietly creep into the warehouse. They start to hunt for the crooks.

They jam open the elevator to catch any crook escaping down the stairs.

Trapper, the expert, goes upstairs. Dodd is a little scared and tiptoes down to the cellar.

On the way he hears a noise. He freezes and holds his breath. But it is only a gurgling pipe.

CLIKON CAMERAS

Down in the cellar, he thinks he has found them. He decides to stand guard until Trapper arrives.

On the roof, Trapper sees that the fire escape is the only way down. He hears voices in the room below.

15

He rushes downstairs and bursts in on the three crooks. But they push him over and escape.

16

One of the crooks heads for the roof and the fire escape. But Pete is waiting for him . . .

17

Another heads for the elevator, but it is out of action and Trapper catches him without any trouble.

18

Now Trapper needs help as the third crook has disappeared. He uses his radio to contact Dodd.

19

Together they search all over the warehouse. Has this crafty villain escaped or is he hiding?

20

They eventually find him in the last place they look. He is hiding in the water tank under the roof.

Who stole the Cadillac?

One day Gloria Burger, wife of the American ambassador, her mother Amy Potts and her son Jimmy Burger, see a crook driving off in their big Cadillac. All three see him and give his description to Detective Dodd: he is short and thin, with dark, curly hair, a black beard and big, bushy eyebrows.

The line-up

POLICE OFFICER

THE MEN IN THE LINE-UP LOOK LIKE PERCY. THEY WERE ALL ASKED TO TAKE PART BY THE POLICE

1 2 3

AMY POTTS

A WITNESS ONLY HAS ONE TRY AT IDENTIFYING THE VILLAIN

GLORIA BURGER

EACH WITNESS SITS IN A SEPARATE ROOM UNTIL IT'S HER TURN TO IDENTIFY THE CROOK

THE SUSPECT'S LAWYER IS THERE. HE OBJECTS TO ANYTHING HE THINKS IS UNFAIR

The police, who think that the villain is Percy Pike, quickly organize an identification parade, known as a line-up. The Burgers and Amy Potts come to identify the crook. But Percy, who is a cunning man, tries to fool them by changing his looks. Which of the men in the line-up is Percy Pike?

AFTER EACH WITNESS, THE SUSPECT CAN CHANGE PLACES IN THE LINE-UP

JIMMY HAS ALREADY IDENTIFIED THE CROOK. HE SITS IN ANOTHER ROOM

A POLICE INSPECTOR IS IN CHARGE OF THE LINE-UP

DETECTIVE DODD STAYS IN THE ROOM HE MUSTN'T TALK OR INTERRUPT

Answers

Percy Pike is crook number 2. To change his looks, he's cut off his hair, shaved off his eyebrows and beard, hunched up his shoulders and put on high-heeled boots. To look fat, he's put on lots of layers of clothes and filled his cheeks with cotton.

Questioning witnesses

As a detective, one of your most important jobs is to question suspects and witnesses. A witness is someone who sees a crook in action and can tell you what happened at the scene of a crime.

Questions to ask

Different witnesses

There are all sorts of witnesses. Some are shy – treat them gently and try to help them. Others get very excited and talk too much. Calm them down so that they tell you only the most important details.

Some, who didn't see the crime at all, just want to join in the action. You must learn to spot storytellers from real witnesses. Remember, if a witness has poor eyesight they may be wrong about the evidence they saw.

It is best to question a witness in a quiet place where you won't be disturbed. Don't hurry her when you ask her questions. Get her to tell you what happened, how close she was, how many crooks she saw and what time it was. Try to find out what the crook looked like.

Did she spot anything unusual about him, such as a limp or a scar? If she saw him clearly enough, ask her to make a quick sketch of him for you. Remember – each witness may tell a different story. You will have to judge who is likely to get it right.

Testing witnesses

Ask the witness to guess how far away something is. This is to find out if she can judge distances.

Ask her to guess how tall you are. If she is right, she will be right about the crook's height.

53

Looking for suspects

When you have questioned each witness, you will have to check their stories and look for the suspects. You need a lot of energy and patience – it is hard work and may take time.

Check all the criminal files in your office. Look for a photo of a crook who fits the description you've been given. If you've found a good set of fingerprints, see if they match up with any in your records.

Remember to check your M.O. file too – you may find a record of a crook who works the same way. Show any identi-sketches of the suspect to people who live or work close to the crime. They may know the crook or have seen him lurking about.

You may find more than one person who fits the suspect's description. Before you question them, find out as much as you can about them. Always remember that many suspects are innocent.

Talk to the suspect's friends. They probably know him best.

You may pick up a few clues about his habits from his work mates.

How does he spend his spare time? Does he go to church or a club?

Find out if he has a criminal record. He may have struck before.

Questioning suspects

There are lots of things a detective should know about questioning a suspect.

Talk quietly and be as patient as possible. Watch out for signs which might help you guess whether he is innocent or guilty. Ask him to tell his story over again – he may slip up and change it.

Signs of guilt

Some guilty suspects look away while you question them, or blush, get hot and angry or grow pale.

But remember – not all crooks show signs of guilt. Some are very good at hiding their feelings.

Signs of innocence

An innocent person may talk too much, not listen to your questions and may get flustered.

He may look worried and unhappy and very uncomfortable as he is feeling very confused.

Most suspects will tell you that they were somewhere else at the time of the crime. This is called an alibi. It is your job to find out if they are telling the truth. It may be very hard to break the alibi of a crook who is used to being questioned.

Checking alibis

Check the suspect's alibi as soon as you can. If he is lying, you will probably spot a mistake in his story. Talk to anyone who may have seen him, but give them a few hints to help them remember.

One suspect said he was watching a film. Make sure he has given you the whole story.

Show his photo to anyone who may have seen him, such as the cinema manager or ticket seller.

Another suspect said he was in the park. Find out what tunes the band played while he was there.

If, as he says, he has lunch there most days, someone must have seen him. Ask anyone you see.

If you are sure a suspect is guilty, go to his house. Tell him you have come to look for the loot.

Don't worry if the crook looks sure of himself. He probably thinks you won't find anything.

Search everywhere. An experienced crook finds very good hiding places for the things he steals.

If you find evidence that proves he is guilty, arrest him. Then take him back to your office.

Warn him that anything he says may be used as evidence. Then write down his confession.

Write to the end of each line so no words can be added. Get him to read and sign each page.

Tracking crooks

A good detective uses his eyes and ears to track down crooks. He trains himself to walk quietly and keep out of sight. And he looks at everything very carefully. Tiny clues, such as a leaf, a broken twig or a matchstick, as well as footprints or trampled grass might tell him where a crook is hiding.

Listen

Stand still and listen for things, such as a snapping twig or startled bird. They might show you where a crook is hiding.

Look

Look all around you – a quick, sudden movement might give the crook away. Remember to keep yourself hidden as well.

Getting used to the dark

Close your eyes for about ten seconds when you go from a light place to a dark one. Then you'll be able to see more quickly in the dark.

Judging numbers

You may have to guess how many people are at the scene of a crime.
If it is a big crowd, try and divide it into a grid of squares with your
eyes. Then count the number of people in one square and multiply
that figure by the number of squares in your grid.

Watching for shadows

On a sunny day, a crook who is hiding behind a tree may forget about
his shadow. He thinks that if he cannot see you, you cannot see him. If
possible, try to position yourself on the sunny side of the tree so that
the crook won't be able to see your shadow.

Hints for detectives

Here is some important information that will help you check a witness's story. Could he have seen the detail he thinks he saw? Is he good at guessing how far away or close things are?

How far away?

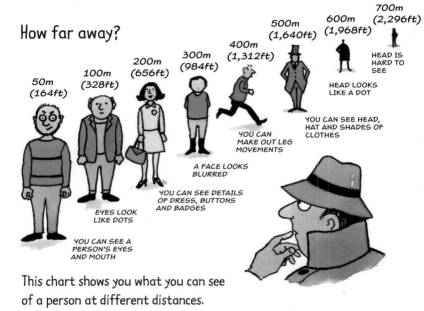

50m (164ft)

YOU CAN SEE A PERSON'S EYES AND MOUTH

100m (328ft)

EYES LOOK LIKE DOTS

200m (656ft)

YOU CAN SEE DETAILS OF DRESS, BUTTONS AND BADGES

300m (984ft)

A FACE LOOKS BLURRED

400m (1,312ft)

YOU CAN MAKE OUT LEG MOVEMENTS

500m (1,640ft)

YOU CAN SEE HEAD, HAT AND SHADES OF CLOTHES

600m (1,968ft)

HEAD LOOKS LIKE A DOT

700m (2,296ft)

HEAD IS HARD TO SEE

This chart shows you what you can see of a person at different distances.

Short distances

MEASURE FROM TOE TO TOE

To calculate short distances, measure the length of your stride. Count your steps as you walk along. Multiply the number of steps by the size of your stride to see how far you have walked.

Things look further away when . . .

YOU LOOK AT THEM ACROSS A VALLEY

YOU ARE KNEELING OR LYING DOWN

YOU LOOK AT THEM DOWN A STREET

THEY ARE IN THE SHADE

THEY ARE THE SAME SHADE AS BACKGROUND

THEY ARE IN MIST OR DIM LIGHT

Things look closer when . . .

YOU LOOK AT THEM ACROSS WATER

THE SUN IS BEHIND YOU

THEY ARE UPHILL OR DOWNHILL

THEY ARE BIGGER THAN THINGS AROUND THEM

THEY'RE ANOTHER SHADE TO THE BACKGROUND

YOU LOOK AT THEM ACROSS A DEEP CHASM

Long distances

POND STREET
1km

Use your watch to work out long distances. If it takes 15 minutes to walk 1km (1,094 yards), you

know that after an hour of walking you'll have covered about 4km (2·5 miles).

How old are they?

If you know the age, height and weight of different people, such as your family, it may help you guess how old, tall and heavy a suspect is. Remember – people change as they grow older. Their hair goes grey or they go bald. Very old people may be wrinkled and sometimes stoop when they stand.

CAN YOU GUESS WHICH OF THE DESCRIPTIONS BELOW FITS EACH OF THE PEOPLE IN THE PICTURE ABOVE?

Jeb is 42, weighs 69kg (152lbs) and is 1.75m (5ft 9ins) tall. Madge is 40, is 63.5kg (140lbs) and 1.6m (5ft 3ins). Albert is 18, is 79kg (174lbs) and 1.9m (6ft 3ins). Jessica is 30, is 51kg (112lbs) and 1.7m (5ft 7ins). Jake is 68, is 100kg (220lbs) and 1.8m (6ft). Hilda is 89, is 40kg (88lbs) and 1.5m (5ft). John is 45, is 80kg (176lbs) and 1.9m (6ft 3ins). Grandpa Peel is 66, weighs 75kg (165lbs) and is 1.8m (6ft) tall.

Answers

5. Jessica 6. Hilda 7. John 8. Madge
1. Jake 2. Jeb 3. Albert 4. Grandpa Peel

Measuring things

It is useful to know how high off the ground certain parts of your body are. Then you can measure the height of suspicious looking things or people without attracting attention.

Height from the ground

TIP OF HEAD

UPRAISED ARM

ELBOW (UP)

SHOULDER

ELBOW (DOWN)

HIPBONE

FINGERTIPS
(HAND DOWN)

KNEECAP

With your feet together, get someone to take your measurements. Remember them so that you can use them in any kind of emergency.

Use your body to measure the height of suspicious things or useful clues. Measure things such as (1) how high a dent is on the side of a getaway car, (2) a broken window, or (3) any odd marks on a door.

Spot the wanted man

On the 12th May, Craig Cregan, the film star, was robbed as he was leaving his home. Witnesses described a man they saw running from the house, and detectives put together this identi-fit picture of the suspect.

The witnesses said the man was between 40 and 45 years old. One of them noticed that he was going bald. The crook was about average height, 1.75m (5ft 9ins), and thin. He was wearing a dark coat, a jumper, scarf and patched jeans. His boots were muddy and he was carrying an old briefcase.

Below are nine photos of suspects taken from detective files. All the crooks look alike but only one of them is the Wanted Man.

Study the photos carefully to see which one it is. The answer is at the bottom of the page.

Answer

No. 1 is too tall and No. 8 too small to be the Wanted Man. No. 5 is too fat, No. 2's face is the wrong shape and No. 9's scar is in the wrong place. Nos. 3 and 6 have the wrong noses and No. 7 has the wrong ears and mouth. The Wanted Man is No. 4. He has grown a moustache but his chin, nose, scar and ears give him away.

Know your crooks

Forgers can be very skilful and sneaky. You will have to work hard to outwit them and trap them.

Counterfeit money

To detect fake money and hunt down the forgers, you will need to use all your senses. You must train your eyes and ears, your nose and fingers. Later you will find some tips on rehearsing your skills.

Fake works of art

CROOK MAKING FAKE 'ANTIQUE' STATUE

HUGE PRICE

Some crooks forge anything valuable, from stamps to paintings.

To detect this sort of fake, you need to know quite a lot about the real thing. (Later you'll find some starting points to help you.)

They'll fake or forge anything they think will cheat people. Here are some examples of their tricks.

Forged signatures

To get people's money, forgers try to copy their writing and the way they sign their names. Later, you'll find out how to study handwriting and detect forged signatures.

Fake clues

A crook may even leave fake clues, or lay false trails, in the hope of fooling you. Even footprints may be faked —if a crook thinks it will help him get away with a crime.

Detecting counterfeits

Forged money, or counterfeit money, is probably the most common fake. Few people realise how many special marks there are on a real bank note, and what a complicated pattern it has. To begin your detective training, check these points on some real bank notes.

First, find the signature and serial number. A real bank note shows the signature of someone important in the bank that printed it.

Each note is numbered in order, as it is printed. (This is the serial number.) If you find two with the same number, then one of them must be a forgery.

Hold it to the light to look for a watermark. This is a pattern pressed into the paper. It looks like a ghostly picture – often a face. It shows up on both sides, but only when the note is held to the light.

In most notes there is also a very thin strip of metal. In the light, it looks like a dark line. Sometimes, in a very tattered old note, you can see it glinting through the paper, where the edge is worn.

Carefully examine the pattern on each side of the note. Use a magnifying glass, if possible. See how complicated the pictures are, and their different shades. Each shade is printed separately onto the paper.

Usually you'll find a picture of someone famous — notice how clearly you can see each hair. You may also find tiny figures in the background and words hidden in the pattern. They are all traps designed to stop forgers making fake bank notes.

Detection training

As a detective, you must be ready to act quickly – you may not have time to examine every note and coin. A good detective can identify fake notes and coins without even looking at them. These pages show some ways to train yourself.

Remember that even the paper used to make money is a special kind – crooks sometimes steal it to make forged bank notes. There may be tiny threads of different shades in the paper, as well as strips of metal. It is so different from ordinary paper that it is possible to detect a real note by the sound it makes when snapped between your fingers. The ink used to print it is special, too – notice the funny smell new bank notes have.

Touch identification

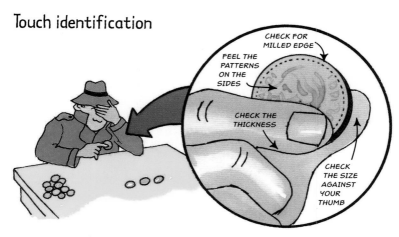

Collect several kinds of coins and test whether you can tell them apart with your eyes closed. Try to place them in order, from the most valuable to the least valuable.

Notice that coins made with some silver often have a milled edge (tiny ridges on the edge). You can feel it if you rub your finger along the edge of the coin.

Money sensitivity training

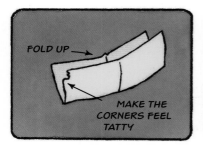

FOLD UP

MAKE THE CORNERS FEEL TATTY

REAL NOTE

1 2 3 4 5

Make some false notes from different kinds of paper, using a real note as a pattern. Fold them up and crumple them, and scruff the corners. (This will make them feel more like real money.)

Number the false notes. Then get a partner to shuffle a real note among them while you are not looking. Try to pick out the real one by touch and sound alone. Then guess the numbers of the others.

Noise identification

You can train yourself to pick out fake coins by the sound they make when they are dropped. To rehearse, work with a partner, like this. One person drops coins

and fakes, one by one, on to a hard, flat surface, such as a table. The other person (with his eyes closed or wearing a blindfold) tries to guess which are fakes.

Inside a forgers' den

This is what detectives Dodd and Trapper found when they broke the Five-Star Forgery Case. It shows what you might find in a forgers' den. The next pages reveal how forgers work.

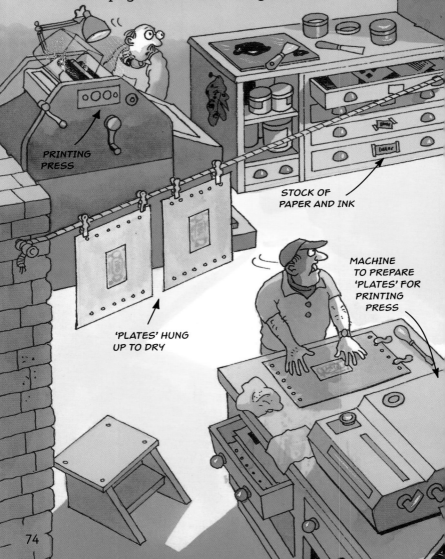

PRINTING PRESS

STOCK OF PAPER AND INK

'PLATES' HUNG UP TO DRY

MACHINE TO PREPARE 'PLATES' FOR PRINTING PRESS

PHOTOGRAPHER'S DARK-ROOM

HIDING PLACE FOR NOTES

THE FORGED NOTES ARE WASHED TO MAKE THEM LOOK USED

PAPER CUTTER

75

How forgers work

Here is the main equipment for making forged bank notes. Examine it carefully so that you will recognize it if you see it. The printing press and camera could be used for innocent business, but a plate or film showing pictures of money is evidence of forgery.

The forger in the dark room is starting on a new counterfeit. He is taking photos of a bank note. (This is against the law.)

Here is the sort of camera forgers like. It can take pictures that show each shade separately, and it uses film as big as a note.

The forger had taken a separate photograph of each shade used on the note, as well as the pattern on the back.

Here is a bit of the film (the photographic negative). Notice that on the negative the pattern is transparent.

PLATE-MAKING MACHINE

PLATE FOUND BY DETECTIVES

This machine shines light through the transparent bits onto a thin metal 'plate'. The light prints the pattern on the plate.

There must be a separate plate for the back of the note and for each shade. (Only one shade can be printed at a time.)

INKING ROLLERS

PLATE

BLANKET ROLLER

PRINTED PAPER

This is the best sort of printing press to use for making money. The ink is put on the plate by the rollers on top.

The inky plate presses the money-pattern onto the blanket roller. The blanket roller prints it on the paper.

Tracking forgers

If you are on the trail of a team of forgers, look first for any building where they would have enough space to work in – and where they could try to hide what they are doing.

Keeping a look-out

GLIMPSE OF LIGHT BURNING THROUGH THE NIGHT

NOTICE THE EXTRA CABLE AND DRAINPIPE

CAR LEFT OUT IN SNOW

Look for suspicious changes in a building, such as new pipes and cables ... or other signs that it is being used for a hidden purpose.

1 CLUES

OILY RAGS

PAPER USED IN TEST RUNS

Look for suspicious rubbish, such as ink-stained rags or badly printed paper.

2

Watch out for any scrap of paper that might show even a tiny bit of money pattern.

If you find a likely-looking site, watch it secretly for a few days to note down suspicious activities. Then look for the clues shown at the bottom of these pages.

LOOK-OUT

LOTS OF TRAFFIC TO AND FROM GARAGE

Notice if the people you see seem to be watchful or suspicious ... and whether there seem to be an unusual number of visitors.

3

Notice whether you can smell printer's ink, or any other strong chemicals.

4

CLICK-CLANK-CLICK-CLANK

Listen for the click-clank noise that means there is a printing press in action.

Forgery smugglers

Forgery is often an international crime. To make counterfeits difficult to trace, they are printed in one country and then smuggled across the borders to another country.

Because of this, detectives from different countries work together. They share information and sometimes they even help customs officers check people at frontiers.

On the opposite page you can see some of the tricks smugglers use. Below you can see how detectives spot smugglers at customs.

Nervousness

TIMID PEOPLE SWAGGER

QUIET TYPES GET NOISY

NOISY TYPES BECOME QUIET

They notice if a passenger behaves in a way that seems out of character. This is how guilty people often show they are nervous.

Luggage tip

BUNDLE OF MONEY IN LINING

CHOCOLATE COATED GOLD BAR

They check the lining in suitcases that seem heavier than the things inside. They examine anything that seems much heavier than it should be. It might be gold.

Smuggling in cars and lorries

THIS CUTAWAY SHOWS HOW MONEY CAN BE SMUGGLED INSIDE A TANKER

PLASTIC BAGS HUNG FROM SUPPORT

NOTES MAY BE HIDDEN IN HOLLOW PARTS OR SECRET COMPARTMENTS IN A CAR. DETECTIVES CHECK FOR THIS BY LISTENING TO THE SOUND MADE WHEN DIFFERENT AREAS ARE TAPPED

SECRET COMPARTMENTS

Behaving strangely

Smugglers like to go through customs with a crowd. They may hang about for a long time, waiting for the right moment – then try to blend in with a group of other passengers.

If they get through customs, they are often so relieved that they give themselves away. They may wink at an accomplice, or smile knowingly – or just act a bit too happy.

Forged paintings

Pictures can be forged too. Some crooks have made fortunes by copying the work of famous painters.

The work of Old Masters (famous painters who lived long ago) is even more valuable. Often many of their paintings have been lost or damaged and so lots of people want to buy what is left.

These pages show some of the signs of an old painting and how they can be faked. On page 84 you can see how fake paintings are detected.

Signs of an old painting

An old painting can show all sorts of long-ago things. The surface has often become dark with age and the paint is also very hard. (It takes about 50 years for oil paint to dry out completely.)

MAGNIFYING GLASS

MAGNIFIED VIEW OF CRACKED VARNISH

If you look closely, you can see that the canvas it is painted on is old, and the frame is old as well. The surface would have been varnished to protect it. Years later, the varnish has become a mass of tiny cracks.

A forger's tricks

One very famous forger worked like this. First, he bought a painting that was very old, but not particularly valuable.

EMPTY FRAME

He carefully took off the paint so that he could use the canvas. (Canvas is tough material, but old age weakens it.)

He studied every piece of work by a certain Old Master, until he knew how to copy every detail.

MINERALS ARE GROUND TO POWDER TO MAKE PAINT

Then he learned how paint was made in the Old Master's time, and mixed it up himself.

He faked a new 'Old Master' and heated it to dry the paint. Then he varnished it and heated it again to dry the varnish.

He rolled the canvas tightly round a tube, to crack the varnish to make it look old. Then he put the canvas back in its old frame.

Detecting a forged painting

When the forger has finished his fake painting, he has to invent a story. Somehow he has to explain how he happened to get hold of this 'famous' work – and why no one has heard of it before. He may have to forge old letters and other documents.

Any of these may be spotted by an expert.

Fake documents

NOTICE HOW PAPER CRINKLES WHEN IT DRIES

Handwriting experts can detect forged writing. Laboratory tests can sometimes even show how old the ink is.

You can make paper look old by soaking it in tea or coffee – try it and see. But it will be blotchy and crinkled.

Fake worm holes

CLOSE UP OF SLICE OF WOOD WITH REAL WORM HOLES

CLOSE UP OF SLICE OF WOOD WITH FAKE WORM HOLES

Sometimes, forgers make fake worm holes in a new frame, to make it seem old.

But holes made by a drill or a needle will be suspiciously straight. Real worms swerve.

The painting itself contains lots of traps too. There may be clues in the canvas, the frame, paint, and the varnish. There are even clues in the dirt on the surface. Scientists can detect modern chemicals from a tiny bit of paint or varnish. They can even work out what made the dust in the cracks.

X-rays

ORDINARY LIGHT SHOWS PAINTING THAT LOOKS VERY OLD

X-RAY PHOTOGRAPH

SHOWS MODERN PAINTING UNDERNEATH

Certain kinds of light rays, such as X-rays, can show up a modern painting hidden under one that looks old.

This is because the light rays show even tiny bits of some shades hidden below, while not showing overlying shades at all.

Nail clue

SUPPORT

BACK OF CANVAS

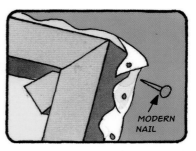

MODERN NAIL

The canvas must be nailed to a frame to make it tight enough for the artist to paint on it.

The nails may reveal when this was done. They weren't machine-made until about 200 years ago.

Find the forger's mistakes

An expert can often detect a faked 'Old Master' by studying the things it shows. This painting was made to look like the work of an artist who lived in Europe 400 years ago. But many of the things it shows do not belong to that time.

There are at least 20 mistakes in the picture. Can you find them? List everything that looks wrong, then turn the page to check. Look carefully and think hard. (You may find you would have made some of the same mistakes.)

The forger's mistakes

All the games and many of the toys in the forged picture are actually copied from a real picture painted by an artist named Breughel. Below are the mistakes the forger made.

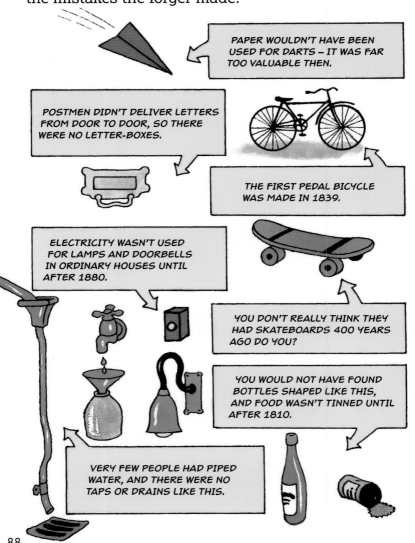

PAPER WOULDN'T HAVE BEEN USED FOR DARTS – IT WAS FAR TOO VALUABLE THEN.

POSTMEN DIDN'T DELIVER LETTERS FROM DOOR TO DOOR, SO THERE WERE NO LETTER-BOXES.

THE FIRST PEDAL BICYCLE WAS MADE IN 1839.

ELECTRICITY WASN'T USED FOR LAMPS AND DOORBELLS IN ORDINARY HOUSES UNTIL AFTER 1880.

YOU DON'T REALLY THINK THEY HAD SKATEBOARDS 400 YEARS AGO DO YOU?

YOU WOULD NOT HAVE FOUND BOTTLES SHAPED LIKE THIS, AND FOOD WASN'T TINNED UNTIL AFTER 1810.

VERY FEW PEOPLE HAD PIPED WATER, AND THERE WERE NO TAPS OR DRAINS LIKE THIS.

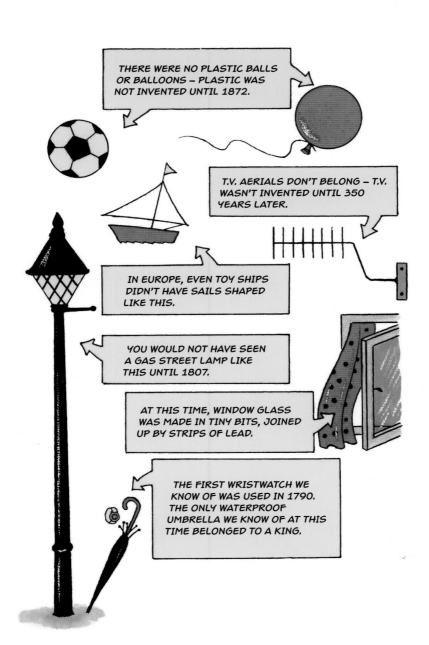

THERE WERE NO PLASTIC BALLS OR BALLOONS – PLASTIC WAS NOT INVENTED UNTIL 1872.

T.V. AERIALS DON'T BELONG – T.V. WASN'T INVENTED UNTIL 350 YEARS LATER.

IN EUROPE, EVEN TOY SHIPS DIDN'T HAVE SAILS SHAPED LIKE THIS.

YOU WOULD NOT HAVE SEEN A GAS STREET LAMP LIKE THIS UNTIL 1807.

AT THIS TIME, WINDOW GLASS WAS MADE IN TINY BITS, JOINED UP BY STRIPS OF LEAD.

THE FIRST WRISTWATCH WE KNOW OF WAS USED IN 1790. THE ONLY WATERPROOF UMBRELLA WE KNOW OF AT THIS TIME BELONGED TO A KING.

Spot the fakes

A gang of thieves stole seven antiques from the shop below. They swapped each with a fake, hoping the owner wouldn't notice how much was gone.

On the right you can see how the shop looked after the raid. How many of the fakes can you spot? (Turn the page upside-down to check.)

These are the mistakes in the fake antiques:

1. The mirror's frame is wrong. 2. The armchair's legs are straight. 3. The tea and coffee pots are different. 4. The knight's suit has the wrong helmet and has lost a gauntlet (metal glove). 5. The candlesticks are different. 6. There are no birds in the case. 7. There is a pot missing from the cardboard box.

Forgers' tricks

One of the hardest parts of a forger's job is tricking someone into buying his fakes. But crooks know a lot of ways to fool people. They know how to make cheap things look valuable, and how to convince people that fake things are real. The tricks shown below have fooled a lot of people.

A good detective should learn as much as possible about tricks like these. Remember – the more you know about how forgers work, the better you will be at detecting them.

Fake discoveries

FORGER CREEPS OUT TO HIDE FAKE COINS NEAR ANCIENT MONUMENT

FORGER DISCOVERS COINS WHILE WALKING PAST WITH GREEDY TOURIST

Sometimes a forger hides things in places where real discoveries might be made.

Then, the next day, he pretends to discover the things he has hidden the night before.

Crooked expert

Sometimes crooks work in teams. One pretends to find something, while the other pretends to be an expert who thinks his 'find' is valuable. (A really crafty crook may pretend to be the world's expert, in hope of keeping people from checking up on him.) Below you can see how a trick like this might work.

Forged signatures

It is almost impossible to sign someone else's name the way they do it. People write their own names (signatures) so often that they do it without thinking. The way they write their signature may become a scribble with a particular shape, or it may have curls and flourishes.

Try to copy a signature and see what happens. Notice how hard it is to make it look natural. Your hand will hesitate, and make strokes that are too light or heavy. You will probably find that the writing looks stiff and shaky, even if you make each letter perfectly.

Look for things like this when you try the puzzle below. Then turn the page to read more about identifying handwriting.

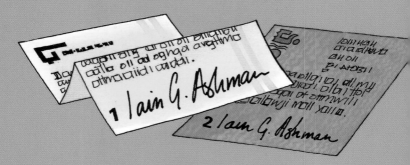

Spot the forgeries

One of the signatures above belongs to Iain G. Ashman. The others are forgeries. They were copied (or traced) by crooks trying to get money from him.

Can you spot the forgeries – and pick out the genuine signature? Compare the writing with the sample at the top of the next page. (The answer is at the bottom.)

Handwriting sample

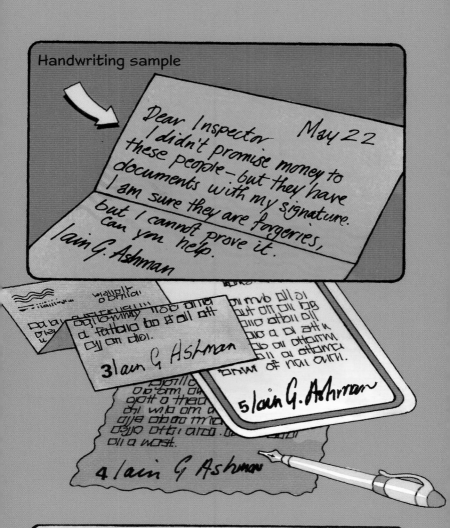

Dear Inspector May 22
I didn't promise money to
these people — but they have
documents with my signature.
I am sure they are forgeries,
but I cannot prove it.
Can you help.
Iain G. Ashman

3 Iain G Ashman

5 Iain G. Ashman

4 Iain G Ashman

Answer

Number 1 is Iain Ashman's signature. Number 5 was traced — notice the short, unconnected strokes, like the lines of a drawing rather than handwriting. The rest were copied.

Handwriting identification

Being able to identify handwriting may help you trace a criminal or find the writer of an anonymous letter. Read the points below and then try the test on the right.

First, notice how the writer makes particular letters. Check whether the letter is always written in the same way. If not, when does it change?

If possible, compare the writing with a sample from someone who uses the same style. This will help you see some of the tiny differences.

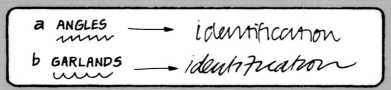

Next, look at how the letters are joined up. (The names of two main ways of joining-up are shown above.) Are they crowded together or strung out? Which way do the letters slant?

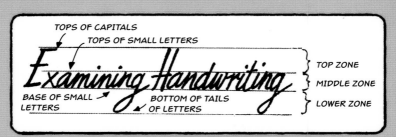

Now draw four lines, like this. The spaces are 'zones'. Compare the size of each zone in different samples of writing.

Handwriting identification test

SENTENCE NO 1
(SIGNED)

SENTENCE NO 2
(UNSIGNED, SLIPPED FACE
DOWN INTO ENVELOPE)

SIGNED SAMPLES

UNSIGNED SAMPLES

You will need:
2 envelopes or small boxes
2 slips of paper for each person who gives a handwriting sample
1 pen or pencil

First, collect samples of handwriting from six people. Ask each
person to copy two sentences on separate slips of paper. Everyone
should use the same sentences and the same pen (or pencil).

One sentence should be signed. This is put in an envelope marked
'signed sample'. The other sentence, written secretly and not
signed, should be slipped face down into a different envelope.
When you have finished collecting samples, shuffle the unsigned
sentences without looking at them. Then try to match them to
the signed samples, and work out who wrote each one.

The case of Miss Atkins's will

When Tabitha Atkins died, aged 92, it was expected that her fortune would go to the cats' home owned by her friend Lucy Potter. Miss Atkins had said so, when she made her will. Everyone knew that she had not spoken to her only relative, John Jasper, for many years.

But when her will was opened, it was found that Jasper had inherited her fortune. Miss Potter told detectives that she believed the will had been forged.

At the top of the next page you can see Jasper and Miss Potter, who both thought they should have the fortune. On the right is the will, spread out to show where the important bits are.

NEWSPAPER STORY PRINTED WHEN MISS ATKINS MADE HER FIRST WILL

The will was typed except for a few lines Miss Atkins added on the last page. The important bits are circled – below, you can read what they say. Do they look suspicious to you? Turn the page to see how this complicated case was solved.

The will

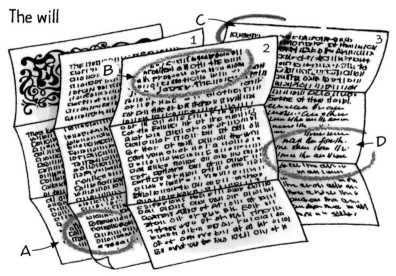

A. Except for the gifts I have put in this will, all of my fortune shall go to the cats at Kitty Korner. It shall belong to them

B. for six months only, and then shall become the property of my nephew, John Jasper

C. forever.

D. To my nephew John Jasper I leave a small token, but he must use my gifts to buy a copy of the magazine 'Kitty Kapers' every month for as long as he lives.

Checking a document

When detectives examined the will, they found that Jasper had forged page 3. He had changed the numbers so that the real page 3 became page 4. This completely changed the meaning of what Miss Atkins wrote. The main part of the will should have said: 'My fortune shall go to the cats at Kitty Korner. It shall belong to them forever.' Here are the clues detectives found.

FORGED PAGE

Watermark

Good stationery often has a watermark that shows what brand it is – you can see it when you hold it to the light. Page 3 had a different watermark from the other pages in the will.

Staple marks

Pages 1, 2 and 4 had two sets of staple marks, showing that they had been stapled together, and then stapled again when page 3 was added. But page 3 had only one set of staple marks.

Forged letter

Jasper had forged the letter 's' in the handwritten sentence on the last page. The 's' was crammed in, and a magnifying glass showed how the ink blurred where it crossed the fold in the paper.

CROWDED LETTER

Notice how the letter 's' is squeezed against the others.

FEATHERY MARKS AND BLOTS

The crease roughens the paper and makes the ink spread out and blot.

FORGED NUMBER

WORN TYPE

Typeface clues

Jasper made the mistake of using a different typeface on the page he forged. If you look at different typefaces, you will see how easily you can tell them apart. With a magnifying glass, you can see how typefaces are slightly different on different computers.

Can photographs lie?

Here are some amazing stories, with photos to prove them. But photos can be changed so they tell a different story.

Turn the page to see.

**MONSTER
BIRD
ATTACKS
LONDONER**

UFO
OVER
CITY

PHOTOGRAPHER SNAPS
MAIDSTONE GHOST

The secret of the Maidstone ghost

FILM

To make the fake ghost picture, we took a photograph of a door. Then we had the film developed.

PRINT

Then we painted a ghostly shape onto the film (try it with poster paints), and had it printed.

Fake UFO

This UFO is just a saucer-shaped metal lampshade. One person threw it into the air while another photographed it, using a fast speed on a camera.

Fake monster bird

This monster bird and its victim were paper shapes, glued to a window. The photographer who took the picture was standing about 1m (3ft) away, inside the room.

Faking monsters

You can use the monster bird trick to photograph fake UFOs, witches on broomsticks, or any flying monster. The windows should be clean, and there should be no lights on in the room, as they might reflect in the window.

Remember that in most cameras, what you see in the viewfinder is a bit different from what the camera 'sees'. This makes it hard to match the paper shape perfectly with the scene outside. So make sure there is a good distance between your paper shape on the glass and the scene beyond it.

Detecting fake photographs

Remember that even a truthful photograph only shows part of a scene. Also, it can give you a false idea of the distance between the things it shows.

When you see a photograph, try to imagine how the scene might have looked if it had been photographed from a different angle. Also, try to work out what might have been happening around it. Below you can see more tricks the camera can play.

Part pictures

Suppose a photograph shows a scene like this. The person on the left looks threatening and the one on the right looks frightened.

But if you could see the real scene, it might look something like this. (A good detective should double-check everything.)

Action pictures

Be suspicious of any action shot that has a black background. This person seems to be making a big leap ...

CAMERA

BLACK CLOTH

But she is really lying on the ground, on a dark cloth. (In a photograph, you cannot be sure which way is 'up'.)

The Case of the Dirty Burglar

This is the scene found by detectives when they were called about the theft of some rare books. The only witness was a guest of the owner of the books. (His story is shown below.) Several clues seemed to show that the burglar had entered and left the room through the window. But the detectives were suspicious. Can you see why?

Turn over to find out how they solved the case.

GUEST

OWNER OF BOOKS

I SURPRISED THE THIEF IN THE ACT. AS I OPENED THE DOOR, I COULD SEE HIM TAKING THE BOOKS, BUT HE RAN TO THE WINDOW AND JUMPED OUT BEFORE I COULD GET A GOOD LOOK AT HIM. ALL I CAN TELL YOU IS THAT HE WAS RATHER A TALL FELLOW.

Detecting fake clues

A good detective should always be on guard against fake clues. A clever crook may have made them to throw you off his track. When you are listening to a story, or examining clues, always ask yourself, "Is it true?" and, "How did it happen?" Remember that you can often solve a case if you know what questions to ask.

Begin by asking yourself what would have happened if you were the crook. Think about each move you would have made. You might even want to go over each step yourself, to find out what clues you should be looking for.

In the Dirty Burglar Case, the trail of footprints was a fake. Below you can see how this was discovered. Now that you know this, try asking some other questions about the case. Check them with the things the detectives asked. See how close you come to the solution.

How did it happen?

To find out whether an outsider would have made the tracks, you have to work out how he might have come through the window. Here are the three most likely ways of getting through the window. But none of them would have made the prints that were found.

Backwards

TOES WOULD MARK WALL →

PRINTS WOULD FACE WALL

How the case was solved

1. How did the thief climb through the window?

2. If he was tall, how could he have jumped quickly through a small window?

3. If he was short, how could he have reached the books without the stool? (His tracks go past it.)

4. How did he know which books were valuable — and how was he able to find them without searching the shelves?

5. If he broke the window from outside, why did the glass fall outside?

6. How could the witness have seen him take the books? (The door would have been in the way.)

7. Why is the witness fully dressed, but wearing slippers?

When the detectives got this far, the witness confessed what he had done. He had muddied his shoes in the flowerbed outside, carried them indoors, and put them under the window. Then he stepped into them, made the tracks, took the books, broke the window, and handed the books and shoes to an accomplice outside.

Forwards (slowly)

WOULD LEAVE TOE PRINTS CLOSE TO THE WALL

HEELS WOULD MARK WALL

Forwards (quickly)

PRINTS WOULD BE FOUND AT A DISTANCE FROM WALL

Fake evidence

'Evidence' is what backs up a story. A good detective always checks that the evidence really fits the story. If it doesn't, it may be fake. Try this test case.

The story

A man who worked for J. G. Jewels claimed he was robbed while taking their money to the bank. Below is the evidence for his story.

The evidence

SCRATCH ON FACE

TEAR IN JACKET

"The money was in my right hand. The thief grabbed me from behind, and put his hand over my mouth so I couldn't call for help."

"Look at the scratch I got from the ring he was wearing. I tore my best jacket trying to stop him, but he still got away."

Cracking the story

Two detectives acted out the story. This showed that:
1. The crook's ring would have scratched the left side of the man's face.
2. The man would probably have torn the sleeve of his free arm (the left) if he had struggled with the crook.

   The man eventually admitted that he had faked the evidence and hidden the money so that he could keep it himself.

Fake accidents

Crooks sometimes make things look like accidents when they were really done on purpose. Study the pictures below to see if the scenes were faked.

The story

In this case, a crook told his insurance company that he had parked his car to look at a cliff-top view, and it accidentally rolled over the cliff. He said that he had just managed to jump out in time. Do you believe him?

Where the car was last seen.

These tracks were discovered near to the edge of the cliff.

Here is a picture of the car at the bottom of the cliff.

Cracking the story

The crook had pushed an old car over the cliff so that he could get insurance money and still keep his own car. These are the clues:
1. A sign shows that the cliff is dangerous.
2. The footprints are deep and point outwards – signs of someone pushing something heavy. Toeprints show where the car began to roll.
3. It was discovered that the crook had taken off the handbrake.

Seeing through disguises

Sidney Lurchpast, a well-known criminal, was able to escape detection for many years by using fake identities and clever disguises. Could you have spotted him?

Below are pictures taken by detectives while on his trail. Some are of Lurchpast in disguise. Some are of innocent people. To work out which is which, think carefully about what can be disguised and what can't. Then turn the page to find out more about seeing through disguises.

Which of these are really of Sidney Lurchpast?

Identifying Lurchpast

Lurchpast was a master of disguise. But if you trace his head and shoulders, you will find they fit into all but the last pictures in each row.

The man in picture 4 has a bigger jaw and a longer neck than Lurchpast, and the man in picture 8 has a smaller ear and a different jaw. These are things that can't be faked or changed.

As a good detective, you should learn to ignore the showy things that can be faked and keep your mind on things that permanently identify people. Below are more of the tricks that Lurchpast used. On the right is another case to test your powers of observation.

The fake identities of Sidney Lurchpast

Lurchpast used lots of actors' tricks. He knew that people often notice how another person stands and moves around.

In one identity, he slouched and swaggered. In another identity, he always stooped a little. Notice what a difference it makes.

Spot the imposters

RODERICK ROEHART   HOUSEKEEPER   UNCLE FOTHERGILL

Here is a photograph of Roderick Roehart, taken just before he set out to explore Brazil. Soon after, his expedition was reported lost.

Years later, when his uncle died, all three people shown below claimed the Roehart fortune. Which could be Roderick Roehart?

Which is the real Roderick Roehart?

HOUSEKEEPER

Obviously, the years have changed Roehart. The hardships he suffered in Brazil have made him thin, bald, and tired.

But you can pick him out from the others by his height, rather short arms, and smallish feet. He is the man on the right.

Finding hidden loot

If a forger suspects you are after him, he may hide evidence or stolen loot in secret places in his house or garden. Here are some things you should know about.

Fake wall clues

You can sometimes detect a hollow wall by the sound it makes when you rap your knuckles on it. Learn the different sounds made when you tap on thick main walls, thin dividing walls, and cupboard walls.

If possible, compare the measurements of the rooms and work out how they fit together. Look for new boards or nails, or fresh paint or plaster, if you think a wall has been boarded up.

DYING SHRUB

WATER TEST

NEW TURF

Buried loot

If you suspect fresh digging, look for new turf – it will be a slightly different shade from the rest. A plant may wilt if its roots are disturbed by digging. Remember that water poured on newly-turned earth sinks in faster than it does in packed earth. (To test this, pour water on a bare patch of ground.)

The Farmhouse Forgery Raid

This lonely cottage was used as a hideout by the gang later known as the Farmhouse Forgers. Thousands of counterfeit bank notes and coins were found in this room. Yet when detectives entered, this is all they saw.

Do you notice anything suspicious? Where would you have started looking for the money? Turn the page for details of the raid.

Discovering the loot

Below you can see the loot found stashed in the cottage and some of the emergency hiding places the forgers used. The forgers were tipped off only minutes before the raid took place. They had to act quickly, hoping the detectives would make only a hasty search. They disguised themselves as an elderly couple to put them off the scent.

The haul

The main part of the haul was found in boxes in the oven. But notes were found under the chair cushions and between the picture and its frame. Coins were found in the flower vases, in the stew, and under the gravel in the fishbowl. Other finds are shown below.

High points of the raid

The pot turned towards the wall held lots of bank notes.

Bundles of notes were also found taped under the table.

But several things looked wrong to the detectives. Did you notice the crooked picture, the agitated goldfish, and the way the flowers were stuffed into the vases? Most suspicious of all, the dog was barking at his 'mistress', and not at the strangers at the door. All this looked very odd to the detectives, so they went ahead and made a thorough search.

Bank notes were found stuffed inside the cut loaf on the table.

Coins were even discovered mixed in the pancake batter.

Famous fakes

Fakes often succeed only because people want to believe in them. Here are some good examples – would they have fooled you? Turn the page to read about one of the most famous fakes in history.

Dr. Koch's sea serpent

From 1845 to 1848, crowds of people paid to see this skeleton. Its owner, Dr. Koch, said that it belonged to a sea serpent. In fact, he had made it himself from pieces of much smaller animals.

Dr. Berringer's fossils

REAL FOSSILS ARE THE REMAINS OF PLANTS AND ANIMALS THAT DIED LONG AGO AND TURNED TO STONE.

DR. BERRINGER BOUGHT THESE FAKE, HAND-CARVED FOSSILS IN 1725, BELIEVING THEY WERE GENUINE.

Fake mermaids

This is one of several 'mermaids' shown in London about a hundred years ago. It is really a stuffed monkey with a fish's tail sewn to it.

DR. BERRINGER WAS SO PROUD OF HIS NEW COLLECTION THAT HE WROTE A BOOK ABOUT IT.

HE REFUSED TO BELIEVE THEY WERE FAKES, EVEN AFTER THE FORGERS TOLD HIM WHAT THEY HAD DONE.

Piltdown Man

A human skull dug up in 1912 at Piltdown in England became world-famous. Experts who examined the skull were very excited – they said it was a two-million-year-old fossil. For forty years it was displayed as the 'missing link' between modern humans and their ape-like ancestors.

In fact, it was a total fake. The skull was not a fossil and the jaw belonged to a type of ape called an orangutan. The pieces had been cleverly matched up and faked to look old, probably by being boiled in a kind of acid. Who the forger was, and why he did it, is still something of a mystery.

Complicated tests were made when the forgery was uncovered in 1953. But one of the most glaring pieces of evidence came from a simple mistake the forger had made – the kind of detail a good detective should have noticed, if he had really looked.

Teeth clue

These are the back teeth of Piltdown Man. As you can see, they slant in different directions. They had actually been filed down to make them look like human teeth. (Apes don't chew their food the way we do, so their teeth do not wear down the same way.) A microscope showed the tell-tale scratches on the teeth tops.

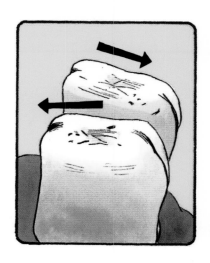

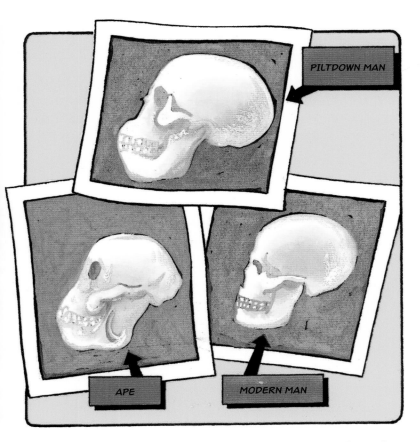

PILTDOWN MAN

APE

MODERN MAN

The top drawing here shows how the bones found at Piltdown were put together. Notice that the main part of the skull looks like a man's, but the jaw looks like an ape's.

Warning!

To be a good detective you should ask yourself, "Is it true? Or could it be a fake?" Think of the tricks you would use if you were a forger.

When the teeth of the Piltdown Man were finally examined, the scratches looked very suspicious. Yet for forty years, no one had bothered to examine them properly.

Know your experts

As a good detective, it is important to know where to go when you need help and who to ask. Below are the names of some useful types of experts. Try to learn to say the names correctly – it will help if you need to ask for information.

Get to know your local library and museums too. Some museums have certain days when they will give you advice on things, or answer questions. The library can help a lot if you learn how to use it.

Handwriting expert – Graphologist

DETECTIVES MAY CALL IN GRAPHOLOGISTS TO BACK UP THEIR CASE IN A LAW COURT

Coin expert – Numismatist

A SET OF MEDALS WON BY A SINGLE PERSON IS MORE VALUABLE THAN SEPARATE MEDALS

If you collect things like stamps or coins, you could make this a special study and become an expert yourself. It may be easier than you think to start a collection.

Take a look at your old toys and comics – some day they may be valuable. In the future, a set of toy models may be all that is left to show the history of cars at a certain time – or of spacecraft or soldiers' uniforms. Try to make complete sets, if you can.

Stamp expert – Philatelist

DISPLAY CASES FOR STAMPS

Plant and animal expert – Zoologist

The Museum Mystery

Early one evening, a tourist wandering around the grounds of the Pharaoh Museum saw a man creeping across the grass. The tourist became very suspicious and so he hid behind a bush.

He took photographs of what the man did next. Look at the pictures he took. Can you put them in the right order to find out what he saw? Was the tourist witnessing a crime? The answer is below.

What the tourist saw

The right order for the pictures is D, G, J, B, E, H, C, A, F, I. The tourist saw a crook stealing a valuable statue from the museum. This is what happened.

The crook crept across the lawn towards the museum (D). He climbed a rope to where the statue was (G). He used his light to find the statue (J). A guard spotted him (B). He escaped down a vine (E). The guard chased him (H). The crook jumped into a car but the guard tried to stop him (C). The crook drove into a bush (A). The guard pulled him out of the car (F). He tied up the crook and telephoned the police (I).

Burglar alarms

To be a good detective and outwit crooks, you have to be very crafty. When you stay in a place you don't know, such as a hotel room, you should set up your own alarm system to warn you of any prowlers.

Bedroom alarms

MIRROR FACING THE DOOR

COAT HANGERS

CRUNCHY PAPER

MIRROR FACING THE WINDOW

Hang a few wire coat hangers on the back of the door. If anyone opens the door, they will jangle loudly. A dog barks a lot if he is woken. Put his basket under the window at night time.

Stand a mirror on each side of the bed so you can see danger points, such as the window and door. Sprinkle crunchy paper on the floor around your bed. They will make a noise if anyone tries to creep up.

The more alarms you set up, the safer you will be. Make one for each door and window in the room. They must be loud so that they frighten crooks away. Here are some simple but noisy burglar alarms.

Tin can alarms

To make a can alarm, put a few stones in a can. Tie string around it. (A) Tie two sticks together and hang the can on them. Lean the sticks against a door. They will crash to the ground if the door is opened.

(B) Hang the can on a door handle. It will slip off if the handle is pulled down. Stand a can on a box. (C) Tie it to a window handle. It will crash down if the window is opened.

Being a detective

Good detectives have to be alert and watchful. They notice everything and are always ready for action. They must be fit so they can chase crooks, and crafty so they can outwit even the most cunning villain. Here are some tips on how to be a good detective.

Notice the smallest hints and clues. Always look out for anything unusual or out of place. Remember, smells and sounds may be clues too.

You should be able to run fast and jump over obstacles in case you have to chase crooks. Running will help to keep you fit and ready for action.

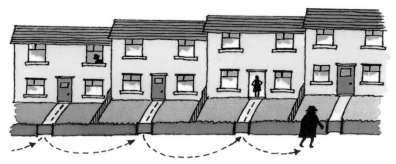

Tracking down crooks can take a long time, but you should never give up. Follow every clue. One might lead you to the crooks' hideout.

Be very patient. Listen carefully to people, even when they talk too much. You never know who might give away vital information.

Try to think fast and act quickly. Put clues together to try to solve a crime. But be very careful not to jump to false conclusions.

Detective training

A good detective can move around houses very stealthily, even at night. He may have to creep up on a crook, and the smallest sound can give him away.

Here is a training course you can set up at home to help you get used to moving silently in the dark.

TRAINING COURSE
STARTS HERE

TRAINER

The course

The course starts at the front door of the house and ends in a bedroom. Arrange some cans, one on top of another, in a wiggly line between the door and the stairs. Fix a piece of string across the bottom of the stairs with sticky tape.

Hang small strips of tin foil over it. Crumple tracing paper or brown paper and put it on one of the stairs. Push two long pins into the frame of the bedroom door at about chest height. Lay a thin stick across them. Put a chair inside the bedroom door.

Training

Do your training at night. Try it with some friends. First everyone walks the course with the light on to learn the way. One detective is the Trainer and stands in the bedroom with his back to the door.

One at a time, the others try to creep up and touch him without being heard. They have to walk between the cans, duck under the string and step over the paper, without knocking down the stick or bumping into the chair.

Each time the Trainer hears a noise he calls out and the detective loses a point. The best detective is the one who loses the least points.

Searching a house

A detective sometimes needs to search a house without being seen or heard. You may be looking for important clues or hidden loot. You can't always be sure that the house is empty, so you have to go in carefully and creep around as quietly as you can.

If you find that there is someone else in the house, you may have to hide quickly. Here are some hints on how to take cover, how to move silently and how to avoid being spotted.

First check a room from outside by glancing through a window.

If there is a pot plant inside the window, use it as cover.

Hold door handles with both hands. Turn them as quietly as possible.

The best way to enter a room is to push the door open with your foot.

If you hear someone coming, hide in a dark, shadowy place.

If there is no hiding place, flatten yourself against a door or wall.

Crawl upstairs so that you can duck quickly if you see someone.

Your shadow can give you away, even if you cannot be seen.

Choose your hiding places carefully. Every bit of you must be covered.

Remember, stairs creak in the middle so keep against the wall.

Has your room been searched?

Detective Dodd is in Paris. He is staying in a hotel and suspects a crook is after some of his documents. To find out if his room has been searched while he is out, Dodd leaves small traps. He makes his room untidy so an intruder won't notice anything unusual.

Here are some ways of finding out if your room has been searched.

Sprinkle a little talcum powder under the window and in front of the door as a footprint trap.

Leave a book open at a special page and lay a hair across it so you can see if it has been moved.

1 Burglar traps

Wedge a paper clip in the door hinge by closing the door. It will drop down when the door is opened.

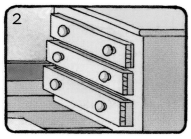

2

Open each drawer by a different amount. Use the width of the front piece of the drawer as a guide.

3

Arrange the envelopes of letters carefully so that each one shows one letter more of the address.

4

Put a few tiny pieces of paper in your letters so they fall out, unnoticed, if anyone reads them.

Turn back a corner of a rug. If a crook looks underneath it, he will lay the rug down flat again.

Observation games

A good detective is very observant, noticing small details which most people would miss. This helps him to find clues at the scene of a crime.

Here are some games to help you improve your observation and memory. They are all designed for three or more players.

Witness game

This is a game for lots of players. One player is the timekeeper and has a notebook and pencil. All the players go outside and stand together on a street corner or outside a shop – but beware of cars. The timekeeper counts to 100 while everyone watches the people on the street.

The timekeeper jots down notes on all the people he sees, what they are doing and what they are wearing. When the timekeeper has reached 100, all the players go home. They write down all the people they saw. The timekeeper looks at his notes to see which player remembers the most people correctly. The player with the best description wins and is the timekeeper for the next game.

1 Spot the changes

2

One player is the shopkeeper and puts a lot of different things on a table. The other players look at them while he counts to 20.

They then turn their backs and the shopkeeper changes some of the things on the table. He takes things away, adds some and swaps some of the things over. The players look again and try to spot the changes.

The first player to spot each one scores a point. Do this four more times. The player with the highest score at the end of five rounds is the winner of the game.

Tray game

One player puts a lot of different things on a tray and shows it to his friends. He lets them look at it while he counts to 40, then he takes it away. Everyone makes a list of all the things they can remember.

The player who can remember the most things wins.

Looking at people

A good detective looks at people carefully so he or she can describe them from memory. This helps them to recognize crooks and tell if they are in disguise. Get used to looking at people. Then turn away and describe what you remember.

Here are the important things to remember.

Try to guess how tall people are. Compare them with others to see if they are bigger or smaller than average. Look at a person's shape. Is he fat, thin or has he got broad shoulders or big muscles?

Try to guess how old a person is. Has he or she got wrinkles? Listen to the way people speak and see if you can guess which country they come from.

Faces are very different. Look carefully at the shape of a person's face, the nose and ears. Note the shade of their hair and eyes and always look out for anything unusual. For example, do they have large earlobes?

Clothes can tell you a lot about people. You may be able to guess what they do from what they wear. Look carefully at details such as hats, ties and scarves, bags and umbrellas.

Always look at people's shoes. Note the shade and whether they are old or new, clean or dirty. Muddy shoes can tell you where someone has been, while clean, shiny shoes can tell you something about the wearer.

Spot the suspicious characters

Detective Dodd is walking down the main street on his way to work one morning. All seems well, but when Dodd looks more closely, he notices several odd things. He alerts HQ immediately.

Study the scene below carefully. How many suspicious characters can you spot and what do you think they are planning to do?

What Dodd notices

The man playing the harmonica has a violin case and the flower van is empty. "Odd," thinks Dodd, "for a crane to lower a bucket over the road. Why isn't the man in the phone booth talking on the phone?"

"That man in the line for the bus and the old lady about to cross the road look suspicious. So do the man in the manhole and the one fixing the street lamp." Dodd sees a security van coming and quickly decides that the crooks are planning to hijack it.

Looking for fingerprints

Burglars have broken into a china shop and detectives are examining the room for clues and fingerprints. Fingerprints are a good clue to a person's identity. They show up best on shiny surfaces.

The scene of the crime

1 Invisible prints

To make an invisible fingerprint show up, sprinkle powder over the place where it might be.

2

Use talcum powder on dark things and cocoa on light things. Brush the powder from side to side.

Sometimes they are hard to see, but even clean hands always leave prints. Can you spot the best places to look for fingerprints in the picture below? Check your answers on page 192.

Keep brushing gently to remove the spare powder. If there is a print there, it will slowly appear.

Now study the fingerprint. Make notes on where you found it, how big it is and what it looks like.

Taking fingerprints

Detectives always take a suspect's fingerprints so that they can be compared with any found at the scene of the crime.

Try taking friends' fingerprints and keeping them in a file. Here is what you do.

KEEP YOUR FINGERPRINT CARDS IN A FILE LIKE THIS

INK PAD

TISSUES

PIECE OF CARD

Make an ink pad with a small piece of soft cloth. Put it on a saucer and pour on some ink.

Press one finger very lightly on the ink pad, as shown. Roll it from side to side.

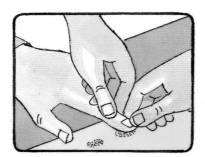

Press the finger firmly on a piece of card. Hold it as shown and roll it from side to side.

The finished fingerprint will be an oblong shape. Take a print of each finger and label it.

Studying fingerprints

Everyone, even identical twins, has different fingerprints. This makes them valuable clues.

Below are the four main types of fingerprint. Study them carefully so that you recognize them when you see them.

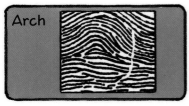

Arch

The shape in this print is like an arch. Notice the scar across it.

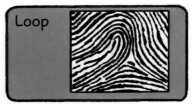

Loop

The line in the middle of a loop is shaped like a bent hairpin.

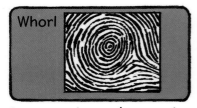

Whorl

One or more lines make a complete circle in the middle of this print.

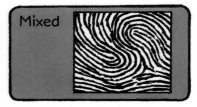

Mixed

This print shows a mixture of the main types of fingerprint.

Fingerprint game

Detectives must be able to match fingerprints exactly to find out who has committed a crime.

This game for four or more people will give you experience of matching fingerprints. Two of the players are suspects and the rest are detectives.

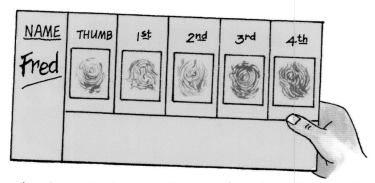

To make a Fingerprint Card, draw lines on a piece of card. There should be six columns — one for a suspect's name and one for each finger.

The two suspects go into a room on their own. They make fingerprints with their right hands on the piece of paper. This is the control sheet.

Each suspect chooses a shade for his fingerprints so he knows which are his later. When they have finished, both suspects wash their hands.

The idea is for the detectives to match the suspects' fingerprints. Each detective needs a Fingerprints Card. The suspects need a big sheet of paper and two paint pads made with different shaded paints.

The suspects take the control sheet to the detectives. Each detective then takes the suspects' fingerprints on his Fingerprint Card. He takes prints of the fingers on their right hands only and makes sure each print is in the right column on his card.

When all the detectives have taken the suspects' fingerprints, they try to match them with the prints on the control sheet. The first detective to match up both suspects' prints wins.

Matching fingerprints

First decide which group each print belongs to (you can see the print patterns on page 149). Then compare the sizes of the prints and how widely spaced the ridges are.

Next look for any small shapes and marks such as scars. Have a notebook and pencil ready so that you can jot down details.

Criminal records

A good detective keeps a criminal record of every crook he catches. Fingers Fred's record shows you the kind of thing you need to know.

Give each crook a number, write down his name and any false names (aliases) he uses, and his date of birth (D.O.B.). Describe what he looks like and take a set of his fingerprints. Find out as much as you can about the crook.

Look at the page opposite to see what Detective Dodd knows about Fingers Fred – how he works, what his hobby is and who his friends are.

Fingers Fred's record

Gestures

Fingers waves his hands when he talks and even more when he lies.

Special features

He was given his name because his finger was bitten off by a horse.

Hobby

Fingers likes to spend a lot of time and money at the races.

Friends

His friends are shady characters, and they all like horse racing too.

Alibi

Fingers always says he was watching television with his mother at the time of a crime.

Routine

He eats chocolates when he's on the job and drops the papers. He always goes out through the window.

Know your territory

As a detective, you need to know your territory – the area you work in – very well, so you can spring into action when a crime takes place. You should know where crooks are likely to strike, where their hideouts are and any getaway routes.

Detective Dodd has been sent to a town he does not know. Here is how he explores it.

Dodd sets off from HQ. He cycles so that he can go slowly and look at everything very carefully.

His first stop is the Public Library. He goes in to borrow a map of his new area.

Dodd cycles along slowly and stops to jot things down in his notebook. He looks at street names and checks them against his map.

He makes a note of where the banks and the expensive shops are.

Dodd chats with local shopkeepers. He may pick up tips about crooks.

He studies cafés. They may have back rooms where crooks meet.

Dodd checks the backs of shops to see where burglars might break in.

He explores alleys, looking out for possible escape routes.

Dodd makes a note of empty buildings where crooks could hide their loot.

When he has finished, he returns to HQ to draw up his own map of the area he has toured.

Danger point map

Here is the map Dodd drew of his new territory.
He has marked all the danger spots with flags.
This will help him track down crooks quickly.

Key

1. A likely getaway route.
2. Possible break-in point.
3. Crooks' meeting place.
4-6. Places that might be robbed.

7. Likely meeting place for crooks.
8. Could be used by crooks as a short cut between Castle Street and Baker Street.

Cover up the key at the bottom of the page and see if you can guess what each flag means. Try drawing a map of your area, starting at your home.

9. Big houses – a likely target.
10. Cars could be swapped here.
11. Concealed short cut – possible escape route.

12. Possible crooks' hideout.
13. Possible crooks' meeting place.
14. Boats could be used for quick escape by river.

Watching crooks

Detectives always want to find out more about a crook's plans. A tip-off from a rival gang may lead the detectives to a secret meeting.

UNMARKED POLICE VAN

USE COVER WHEN POSSIBLE

REMEMBER TO ACT NORMALLY

USE DISGUISES

TRY NOT TO BE NOTICED

Here are some ways of secretly keeping watch on crooks and their contacts, and of listening to them talking and hatching their plans.

Ghosting

Detectives often 'ghost'. This means watching people or buildings without being seen. Here is how to ghost near crooks' hideouts and meeting places to overhear conversations and plans.

Walking the dog is a good excuse for ghosting. Stop every now and then to pat it or talk to it.

Go ghosting with a friend. If you see anything, stop and pretend to be deep in conversation.

Carry an empty suitcase as if it was very heavy. Keep stopping to put it down and rest.

Pretend you are lost. Hold a piece of paper and scratch your head when you look at house numbers.

Keep close to walls in narrow streets and avoid street lights.

Wear soft-soled shoes and creep along, keeping your head down.

If you are by a window and someone suddenly looks out . . .

bend down quickly and pretend to be tying your shoelace.

If you have to pass an open door, look to see if the coast is clear . . .

then tip-toe past it as quickly and as quietly as you can.

Bank raid

Detectives have been tipped off about a bank raid. They quickly arrange a stake-out. A stake-out is a police trap. The detectives disguise themselves.

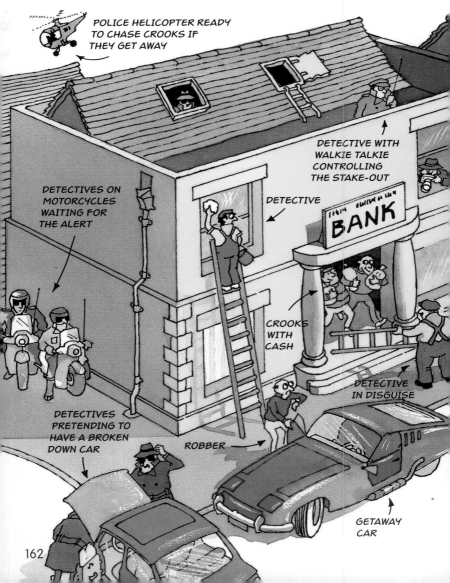

POLICE HELICOPTER READY TO CHASE CROOKS IF THEY GET AWAY

DETECTIVE WITH WALKIE TALKIE CONTROLLING THE STAKE-OUT

DETECTIVE

DETECTIVES ON MOTORCYCLES WAITING FOR THE ALERT

BANK

CROOKS WITH CASH

DETECTIVE IN DISGUISE

DETECTIVES PRETENDING TO HAVE A BROKEN DOWN CAR

ROBBER

GETAWAY CAR

They take up their positions near the bank and wait for the signal for action. Can you work out what happens next?

UNMARKED POLICE CAR

DETECTIVES DRESSED AS OLD MEN

POLICE VAN FULL OF DETECTIVES AND DISGUISED AS ICE CREAM VAN

DETECTIVE PRETENDING TO MEND ROOF

What happens

As the robbers run out of the bank, the window cleaner blocks them with his ladder. The workman on the roof opposite signals the detective on the bank's roof, who calls the police bikes. Getaway routes are blocked by the broken-down car and caravan. The crooks are caught.

163

The chase

When a crime takes place, detectives need to act quickly. They must find the crooks' getaway route and try to guess where they are going. If they guess right, they will be able to cut off the crooks' escape.

1

A watch shop has been broken into. The alarm has gone off and detectives rush to the scene.

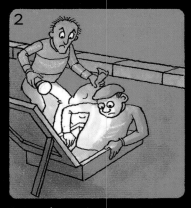

2

The crooks escape through a skylight. They run across the rooftops and enter another skylight.

3

The detectives find the second open skylight, but the crooks have already reached the fire escape.

4

The crooks escape on the getaway motorcycle they have left at the bottom of the fire escape.

They head for a patch of wasteland and swap the bike for a stolen car they have waiting.

The crooks' stolen car is spotted by a policeman on duty. He tells HQ which way it is heading.

Further on the crooks are stopped by a roadblock. They abandon the car and run to a river nearby.

They steal a boat and set off for the port. But the detectives find the car and are soon on the trail.

The crooks reach the port. Thinking they are safe, they creep towards a boat that is about to leave.

But as they board the boat, the detectives are waiting for them. There is no way of escape.

Call-up

When the burglars break into the watch shop, an alarm sounds in the control room at Detective HQ. The radio operator immediately starts a call-up, calling every detective with a radio in the area. He says where the crime was and which way the burglars are heading. All the detectives then start closing in on the crooks.

It is important that everyone acts fast. On the next page you can see who goes into action.

Radio control room

Call-up alphabet

Radio calls must be very clear. Use this international call-up alphabet when you spell names or car numbers. Each word stands for a letter of the alphabet and is easy to hear.

A – Alpha	G – Golf	M – Mike	S – Sierra	Y – Yankee
B – Bravo	H – Hotel	N – November	T – Tango	Z – Zebra
C – Charlie	I – India	O – Oscar	U – Uncle	
D – Delta	J – Juliet	P – Papa	V – Victor	
E – Echo	K – Kilo	Q – Quebec	W – Whisky	
F – Foxtrot	L – Lima	R – Romeo	X – X-ray	

Detectives on foot patrol are alerted and head for the scene of the crime.

Detectives in cars will try to spot the getaway car and trail it. They keep a safe distance.

Local police stations are called up. They set up road blocks.

The river police are alerted in case the crooks try to escape by boat.

Airport police are told to look carefully at all people leaving the country by plane.

Port police are warned to keep a close watch on everyone near the boats.

Information room

When you are after a gang of crooks, set up a special room where you collect all your information. Find out how the crooks work and where they usually strike so that you can track them down.

The information room below has been set up to catch a gang of car thieves.

THESE DRAWINGS OF THE SUSPECTS ARE BASED ON WHAT WITNESSES SAID THEY LOOKED LIKE.

INFORMATION DESK

MESSAGE TRAY

1 Information sources

THE MEN AT THIS DESK SPEND A LOT OF TIME ON THE PHONE. THEY ANSWER CALLS FROM PEOPLE WHO THINK THEY HAVE SEEN SOMETHING SUSPICIOUS. EACH MESSAGE IS TAKEN TO THE OFFICER.

MEMBERS OF THE PUBLIC CALL TO REPORT THEIR CARS HAVE BEEN STOLEN.

Escorting a V.I.P.

A good detective sometimes has to escort V.I.P.s (Very Important People) from one place to another. The detective is one of a team that surrounds the V.I.P. and protects him from attack or kidnapping.

This foreign statesman is visiting an embassy and has asked for a police escort. You know that he will be in greatest danger when he leaves his car. In the picture below you can see how the team should work.

MOTORCYCLE ESCORT BEHIND THE V.I.P.'s CAR

V.I.P.'s BULLETPROOF CAR

171

Escorting valuables

Detectives escort valuables and money to and from banks. Sometimes people lie in wait, ready to pounce, so even the best detective has to be very careful.

If you carry valuables from one place to another every day, try to vary your route. That way it will be hard for anyone to watch you. It is also a good idea to make the trip at different times of the day if you can. You must not attract attention, so act as naturally as possible.

Here are some more tips on what to do.

Before you leave HQ, write a note. Give your route and say when you expect to reach the bank.

Hide the valuables at the bottom of a shopping bag so that no one suspects what you are doing.

When you leave the building, use the stairs and not the elevator. You can be trapped in an elevator.

Keep close to buildings when you walk along the road. Then you are safe from people in cars.

Steer clear of danger points along your route — such as doorways and the entrances of garages or narrow alleyways. And remember that crooks often lurk behind trees or in thick bushes.

Remember not to walk too close to high walls. You never know what is on the other side of them.

Avoid lonely spots and be very careful in places where you can't see the road ahead of you.

Avoid crowds. They slow you down and make it easy for a crook to grab your bag and valuables.

Things can go wrong even when the bank is in sight. Walk at a normal speed, but be ready to run fast.

Which is the safest route?

Mrs. Hill is old and lives alone. She wants to take her valuables to the bank. She is going to walk there but is frightened someone might try to rob her.

Can you choose the safest route for her by looking at the picture below? The answer is on page 192.

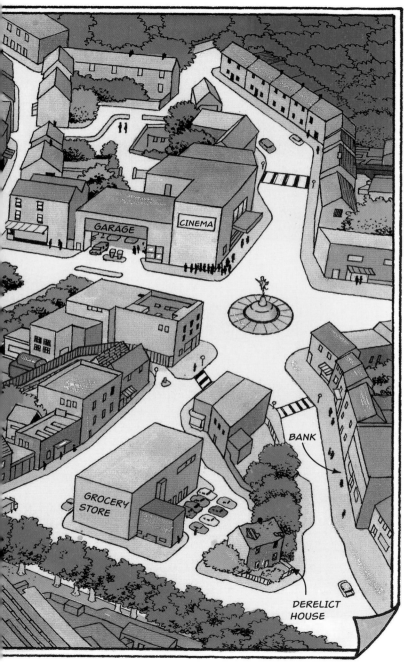

GARAGE

CINEMA

BANK

GROCERY
STORE

DERELICT
HOUSE

175

Finding the hideout

When a crook knows detectives are looking for him, he hides in a place where he thinks they will not find him. But a good detective keeps watch on the crook's friends. They may lead to the hideout.

Here are some of the suspicious signs to look for.

The crook's sister starts buying twice as much food as usual. Who is eating it all?

One of the crook's friends buys cans of dog food, but he has not got a dog. Whose dog is he feeding?

Watch the crook's friends when they go out in the evening. Make sure they do not see you. If they head for a deserted spot, follow close behind them to find out where they are going.

Daytime house

Keep a close watch on houses where you think the crook might hide.
Look out for suspicious signs, such as a lot of extra washing on the
line. And why are these window blinds drawn during the day?

Night-time house

Night time is a good time for spying on houses. There may be a lot of
people in this house because all the lights are on. A lot of visitors could
mean the crooks are meeting there.

After the crime

A thief often gives himself away after a crime.
Excited by his success, he forgets to act normally.
A good detective spots these changes at once.

Here are some of the mistakes Slippery Sid
makes after he has been involved in a burglary.

Sid starts spending a lot of money at the most expensive shops in
town. When he goes shopping he pays for everything in cash.

Sid has always been very stingy with his money. But he suddenly decides
to give a big party and invites all his friends to his house.

Sid's girlfriend, Selina, is thrilled with her presents from him. She puts them all on at once and shows them to her friends.

Sid doesn't have a steady job. But now he has bought himself a very expensive foreign car and drives around showing it off.

Sid usually goes to visit his mother. This year he is taking Selina to Spain where he has rented an expensive villa for a week.

Searching a suspect

Detectives often have to search a suspect for goods they think he has stolen. This is called 'frisking'. Here are the main things to remember when frisking someone.

DON'T FORGET THE ARMS, THE SUSPECT MAY HAVE SOMETHING TIED TO THEM

ALWAYS LOOK UNDER A SUSPECT'S HAT AND IN HIS GLOVES

CHECK THERE IS NOTHING HUNG ROUND HIS NECK

HIS LEGS MAY HAVE OBJECTS STRAPPED TO THEM

CHECK INSIDE TROUSER CUFFS AND UNDER THE INNER SOLES OF SHOES

Get the suspect to face a fence or wall. He should be bending forwards with his face down and his hands flat against the wall. This way he can't attack you. Now quickly pat all the way up his sides and arms.

Start with the ankles and work upwards so you don't miss anything. Next check his pockets and all the danger points above.

Looking uncomfortable

Some crooks try to hide things under their arms. This isn't easy.

False heels make walking difficult for someone not used to them.

Suspicious bulges

Bulges may indicate secret pockets. You should investigate.

Looking hot

Why is this man wearing a huge coat on a hot summer's day?

Fake injuries

Look closely at lumpy bandages. They may be hiding something.

Pram trick

Beware of people pushing empty prams. What are those bulges?

Making an arrest

All detectives can arrest suspects. If you have evidence that someone has committed a crime, you can arrest him and take him in for questioning.

Here are some of the things to remember.

You must have a good reason for making an arrest. If you suspect someone is a thief, watch him carefully before arresting him.

Always warn a suspect that anything he says will be written down and may be used as evidence against him. It is a good idea to have a friend with you when you do this. Then you have a witness to help you.

If your suspect struggles to get away, don't hit him. Try to knock things out of his pockets. He will be confused and try to pick them up.

Useful armholds

This is the normal armhold to use when you take a suspect to HQ.

If he struggles a bit, try using this stronger type of armhold.

Use these armholds on strong people who struggle a lot. Try them out carefully on your friends first and see if they can get away.

At the hideout

Detective Dodd's dog has tracked some crooks down to their hideout in the country. The crooks have just carried out a big burglary and are lying low.

LOOT COULD BE LOCKED IN HERE

KEYS

DODD WATCHES THE ROOM. WHEN THE CROOK TURNS HIS BACK, DODD WILL SIGNAL TO TRAPPER

1 What happens

At the signal, Detective Trapper throws a stone into the bushes. The crook on guard hears it.

2

He goes to look at the bushes. Trapper jumps up and grabs him from behind and arrests him.

They're waiting until the search for them is called off. But their luck has finally run out. Here's how Detectives Dodd and Trapper arrest them.

DETECTIVES' VAN HIDDEN BEHIND BUSHES

THIS CROOK IS CHECKING THAT THE COAST IS CLEAR

TRAPPER WAITS FOR THE ALERT FOR ACTION

The second crook wanders out to see where his friend is. He tries to run but is caught by Dodd's dog.

The one crook left is too sleepy to fight or run away. There is no escape so he quickly gives in.

Theft at the manor

A famous painting is missing from the Portrait Room of Oakwood Manor. Detectives search the grounds of the manor and find the frame of the painting behind the hedge under the Portrait Room window. They question everyone who was in the manor or its grounds at the time of the theft.

WILLOW TREE   WEIR

JETTY

JETTY

PORTRAIT ROOM

MANOR HOUSE

PRIVATE GARDENS

FOOTBRIDGE   SHRUBBERY

Detective Dodd decides there are five people who could have stolen the painting. He takes a statement from each of them and finds that two are lying.

Below is an aerial view of Oakwood Manor. Study it carefully and then read the suspects' statements on the next page. Which of the suspects is lying?

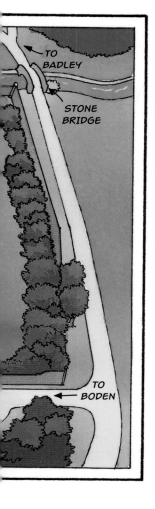

TO BADLEY

STONE BRIDGE

TO BODEN

Plan of the manor

WINDOW

PAINTING   ENTRANCE   STAIRS
            HALL

Scene of the crime

PAINTING WAS HERE

The suspects' statements

The five suspects are an artist, a hiker, an angler, a gardener and a cyclist. Detective Dodd questions each of them separately.

Here are the suspects' statements. Read them carefully. When you think you know who is lying, turn the page to find out what really happened.

Artist's statement

Dodd: "You say you were sketching alone in the Portrait Room just before the robbery. You went into the next room for a few minutes and when you came back you found that the painting had gone."

Artist: "Yes. A hiker came into the Portrait Room and asked me about a picture in the next room. I went to look at it with him. An attendant was also looking at it. As I was talking to the attendant, the hiker left us. When I returned to the Portrait Room I saw the hiker leaving. The picture had gone and I called the attendant."

Hiker's statement

Dodd: "You say you are on a walking tour but you are not carrying a map. Did you visit the Portrait Room at the manor?"

Hiker: "Yes. There was an artist sketching. I asked him about a picture in another room and we went to look at it. He started talking to an attendant so I picked up my rucksack and left. I did have a map, but I lost it this afternoon. I was leaning over a stone bridge watching an angler in trouble. My map fell into the river and floated away under the bridge. I must remember to buy a new one."

Angler's statement

Dodd: "You say you were fishing by the willow tree. You hooked a log which dragged away your rod. I know the river. Why didn't you run to the jetty on the bend and wait for it there? And why were you in the private gardens?"

Angler: "I ran to the bend but tripped and got there too late. Then I saw the log under the manor jetty so I crossed the bridge and went through the gardens to get to it."

Gardener's statement

Dodd: "You were cutting the hedge in front of the Portrait Room window. At about the time of the crime you picked up a sack and ran to the private gardens. There you gave the sack to an unknown man. Why?"

Gardener: "The sack was for the hedge clippings. I ran to the private gardens because I saw a stranger there. He said he was an angler and his rod was under the jetty, so I lent him the sack to kneel on."

Cyclist's statement

Dodd: "You say you are going to Boden. At Badley you told the police that some things had been stolen from your bicycle. Badley is a short distance away but you left there an hour ago. Why has it taken so long and why did you leave the main road?"

Cyclist: "This way is a short cut and I wanted to arrive before dark. Stopping to mend a puncture slowed me down."

Dodd: "The Badley police say they have found your lamp and pump."

189

Who stole the painting?

The picture was stolen by the hiker and the cyclist. The hiker lied about the map floating under the bridge. The weir in the photograph shows that the river flows the other way. It had carried the angler's rod and line towards the private gardens.

The cyclist lied about the puncture. He could have mended one, but could not have pumped his wheel up because his pump had been stolen.

Below you can see how the crime was carried out.

The cyclist arrives at the manor early. He hides between the hedge and the Portrait Room window.

The hiker is pretending to look at pictures. He asks an attendant to explain something to him.

Then he asks the artist to come too. He leaves the two talking and sneaks off to the Portrait Room.

Now the Portrait Room is empty. The hiker hurries across to the window and pushes it open.

The hiker makes sure no one can see him. Then he lifts the famous painting down from the wall.

He slips the painting through the open window to the cyclist, who is hiding outside.

The cyclist stays in his hiding place. He carefully cuts the painting out of its frame.

Then he rolls it up and hides it up his sleeve. He heads for the bushes where his bicycle is hidden.

He takes the seat off the bicycle and slips the rolled up painting into the bicycle frame.

Then he puts the saddle back and pushes the bicycle back to the road. There detectives stop him.

Answers

Answer to Looking for Fingerprints on page 146.

In the picture above, the red circles indicate the best places where you should begin your search for any fingerprints.

Answer to Which is the Safest Route? on page 174.

The green line shows which route is the safest. It is long but avoids all the danger spots and leads past safe places such as the playground and the police station. The red stars show the danger spots. You can check why they are dangerous on pages 172–173.